TRUE WEALTH STARTS IN THE MIND

Whatever a man puts his MIND
on will not be denied him

LISA M. JONES

For information regarding special discounts for bulk purchases, please contact the publisher:

LaBoo Publishing Enterprise, LLC
staff@laboopublishing.com
www.laboopublishing.com

Scripture quotations marked (NIV) are taken from the Holy Bible, New International Version®, NIV®. Copyright © 1973, 1978, 1984, 2011 by Biblica, Inc.™ Used by permission of Zondervan. All rights reserved worldwide. www.zondervan.com

Scripture taken from the New King James Version®. Copyright © 1982 by Thomas Nelson. Used by permission. All rights reserved.

The Holy Bible, King James Version. Cambridge Edition: 1769; *King James Bible Online*, 2019. www.kingjamesbibleonline.org.

TABLE OF CONTENTS

FOREWORD

Growing up in the '70s I would frequently hear on commercials that a mind is a terrible thing to waste. It was a cute catchphrase for many, but forty-plus years later that phrase still rings true as the cornerstone of how I now live my life. I've learned that controlling one's mindset is the key to controlling the quality of life that one lives. The mind is a powerful gift that God gave to each of us. The challenge is learning how to control it so that it releases all of the obvious and hidden treasures that God has promised us.

In her collaborative effort titled *True Wealth Starts in the Mind*, Lisa M. Jones and her group of handpicked, amazing contributing authors, have done just this. They have provided the reader with a roadmap and the keys to unlock the secrets to the accumulation of wealth.

One of the things that I find extraordinarily special about this book is the selection of contributing authors. They vary widely in backgrounds, age, race, gender, and creed, but they all have this one thing in common: They have learned to master their mindsets and create lifestyles that others admire and desire. Using their personal stories of tragedy and triumph, heartbreak and joy, these varied authors rose from very humble beginnings that included, single motherhood, the foster care system, physical abuse, and poverty to become a part of the elite 2% of the income earners in this entire country. The reality is that success leaves clues. True Wealth does start in the mind and this book provides the clues to not only attaining wealth, but creating a lifestyle of spiritual, mental, physical, emotional and financial prosperity. Enjoy!!

Andrea L. Jackson

INTRODUCTION
WHATEVER MAN PUTS HIS MIND ON, IT WILL NOT BE DENIED HIM

In Genesis 11, God declares: *Whatever man puts his mind on will not be denied him.* Looking back over my life, I can see how I exercised this principle without knowing what I was doing. The mind is a powerful machine. It can cause one to win big or fail drastically. After years of personally developing through reading, attending events, listening to great speeches, saying my affirmations, being intentional about what I spoke into the airways and encouraging others, my mindset changed drastically.

Fix your mindset about how you see life, love, friendships, money and success and you can live a lifestyle beyond your wildest dreams.

I grew up in inner city Baltimore and I was blessed to be raised by two amazing parents. Although outside our home the environment wasn't always positive, my parents managed to protect us from our surroundings and made sure we weren't a product of our environment. They had very strong views on how children should be raised, and they stuck to each one of them. We were never allowed to stay over at friends' homes, we had to be in the house when the sun went down, and we were taught to mind our own business. We were taught to respect our elders, eat dinner as a family, pray together, have Bible study together, sing together, play board games as a family and we teased/laughed at each other quite a bit. We were instructed to stay close and protect each other. We didn't have a lot but due to the love and warmth of our home we felt rich.

When I reached my teenage years, I began to see the world differently. There were families that lived a different lifestyle than ours. They had money and material possessions that we didn't have. I couldn't understand how the God I believed in and served would say let this group of people succeed and this other group fail. I questioned, what were the differences between them and us? I wondered how to make the adjustments so I could have more. I had so many questions.

After high school, I had to decide what I wanted for my life. I needed to discover who I was and why was I here. THE TWO GREATEST DAYS IN YOUR LIFE are the day you are born and the day you find out why. Learning one's true identity is difficult and I wasn't sure how to start the process of figuring out who I was. The only place I knew to start was in a book. Reading will cause one to grow in all areas: Spiritual, Mental, Physical, Social and Financial. I understood by reading new information, I could eliminate or adjust the old information. I started reading all types of self-help books, I meditated on the Word of God, I recited my affirmations daily and I started listening to sermons from different spiritual leaders while praying for answers. If you change the way you see things, the things you see will change. God will honor his word and he said, if you SEEK, you will find. He said if you KNOCK, the door will be open and he said if you ASK, the answer will be given unto you and you will receive. I did all of the above and it worked. I became obsessed with researching and seeking out successful people. I wanted to learn what the commonalities of successful and wealthy people were and how as a single African American mom with a six-year-old child could utilize the same principles and move from vision to reality.

I noticed that wealthy people talked differently, thought differently, worked differently and associated themselves with different types of people. They sought out people that were like-minded and they walked in total expectation. They expected to win, to be rich, and to be financially independent. I figured out that successful people and unsuccessful people actually dislike doing the same things. The difference between the two types of people is that successful people do it anyway. They embrace the challenges and conquer their fears. They will do whatever it takes to win. They know how to play hurt and they never take on a victim mindset. I wanted to adopt this mentality and therefore, I needed to start spending time around wealthy people.

I admired the men and women I listened to and read about. I admired their mindset. They controlled their thoughts, which ultimately controlled their actions. The glass was always half full. They never had a bad day; they had bad hours but never a whole day. They were optimistic and believed that the possibilities existed. They didn't do everything right and all the plans weren't always victorious, but they never ever quit. They understood that winners never quit, and quitters never win. Almost everybody quits. Almost everybody gives up and listens to the naysayers, but not winners. They are willing to work hard so that one day they will be in a position to play hard. They know who they are and where they're going. They build by design and not by default.

In building my business, I went through the three stages that all new businessmen and women go through. I went through the Discovery Stage, the Development Stage and now I am proud to say, I made it to the Advisory Stage. Once you discover who you are and what you want, you are now ready to be developed into the superstar you were created to be. The development stage can take years because more often than not, we have to make mental shifts from wrongful thoughts and inaction to the right thoughts and action. In my development stage, I was a player and I didn't overthink everything. I didn't always understand the play that was called but I trusted my leaders. The word of God says the MEEK shall inherit the earth. The word meek means the learned one. The meek are always learning. I am always willing to learn and get better. I walked with an attitude of gratitude. I had the utmost respect for all who were willing to teach me the mindset of the wealthy.

Because we have been conditioned from a very early age to think a certain way and given faulty information to support those beliefs, it is crucial that during the development stage, reprogramming takes place. In order to reprogram my mindset, it was time for me to seek out some wealthy mentors.

SHIFTING MY MINDSET

Do not be conformed to this world, but be transformed by the renewal of your mind, that by testing you may discern what is the will of God, what is good and acceptable and perfect.
English Standard Version, Romans 12:2

Once I found the mentors, I started duplicating them and that was the beginning of an amazing shift in my mindset. I noticed that wealthy people had a few things in common. They made themselves **AVAILABLE**, they are very **ACCOUNTABLE**, they take full **RESPONSIBILITY** for their outcome and they are **VULNERABLE**.

The first thing I did was make myself available. If I was going to make the necessary adjustments mentally, I needed to be available to hear the messages these men and woman were sharing. I attended every conference, workshop, conference call and locker room session they hosted. In doing so, my belief system and confidence level increased and suddenly the excuses I used to use to support my lifestyle of lack were gone. I was strengthened each time I heard the messages they shared.

I was booked to speak at a government agency for Black History Month and my topic was Economic Empowerment. Before the workshop, I decided to interview a very successful leader and I asked him the difference between rich people and poor people. He answered my question immediately without hesitation. "Lisa, that's an easy question. The difference is poor people don't go to the meetings." I was so surprised to hear his response. He said rich people will drive for hours to attend a meeting that will show them how to get better so they can grow mentally. Poor people give the job the best hours of their day and when it's time to better themselves they are tired. They conform to their environment and never seek out a better way. I was determined to find a better way. I made myself available.

While building my business I attended meetings every week and I talked to my mentors daily. I stayed humble and coachable so they would feel good about coaching me. If you're not available, how will you learn or build your confidence level? Availability is a key component in order to be successful in any area of your life. If one joins a gym, it will never work if you don't make yourself available to go back and workout. If you're hired for a job, you must make yourself available to work the scheduled hours. If you want success, you must make yourself available. Success is jealous. You can't date it or string it along; you must marry it. Are you available for success? Is what you are doing getting you closer to your goals and dreams or pulling you farther away? When you study the lives of wealthy men and women, they do their due diligence and they are always available for success.

Next, I stayed ACCOUNTABLE. I never took the risk of leaning to my own understanding. I knew that I didn't have all the answers, so I called my mentors daily. They had the ability to see farther than I could, so I trusted them and their recommendations. You can't be in a position of authority without being accountable. Immature people hate accountability and those who want more embrace it. I never wanted to be one of the ones who were always starting to start something. These folks are vision rich and execution poor, due to lack of accountability. Accountability will force one to act and not procrastinate. There's nothing like being accountable to a leader who has your best interest at heart and who has a vested interest in your success. But be careful in selecting an accountability partner. Make sure the one you are accountable to is wise and can give good counsel.

*Again, I say to you, that if **two** of you shall **agree** on earth*
as touching anything that they shall ask,
it shall be done for them of my Father which is in heaven.
King James Version, Matthew 18:19

I internalized this scripture and believed it. Those who understand it will understand the power of accountability. I figured out that the same mindset, actions and inactions that got me into my mess and undesirable lifestyle would not get me out. I needed a truth teller in my life that would give me correction, protection and direction. Personally, I love accountability because I never wanted to try and figure it all out by myself. I didn't have to create my own footprints. All I needed to do was to walk in the footprints of those who had gone before me. They tested the road less traveled and figured out a strategic game plan to get from A to B. I just needed to duplicate their actions and I should realize the same outcome. No time for overthinking this game called wealth. I just needed to take on the mindset of the wealthy, personalize it to fit into who I was and run the play. Once I became a better version of me, running the play was easy. Coaches call the play and players run the play.

Successful people take responsibility for their success. I took full responsibility for my outcome. I told myself daily, *if it is to be it is up to me.* They seek out qualified opinions and they refuse to listen to folks that aren't future focused. They speak what they seek until they see what they speak.

Often you will find people who get stuck in their past. I was diagnosed with stage 4 cancer eight years ago. It was the most traumatic experience I had ever endured. I was so bad off that I really didn't think I would make it through. At one point I had planned my homegoing service because I didn't want my daughter or parents to go through that process. I was giving up and failing fast. I couldn't hear from God because I took my eyes off the solution and put them on the problem. All I could see was the pain, the weakness, the treatments and the negative diagnosis. I forgot about the faith that carried me through so many other challenges. Then one day my friend Mike Evans called to check on me and after hearing my pain, fear and weakness he decided to speak life into my situation. He said, "Lisa, let me remind you of who you are. Let me remind you of the lives you have touched, the stages you stood on, the success you accomplished, the vessel you are, the power in your speeches and the future that's before you." That phone call caused a shift in my mindset and suddenly I developed the need to live. I wanted to live. I wanted to experience the things Mike reminded me of again. I wanted to live for my daughter, my parents and my organization. I decided to take responsibility for my life and fight for my healing. I reconnected to my source, my Lord and Savior Jesus Christ, and I started claiming the victory. I changed my language and even though the pain was unbearable at times I kept singing and praising His name. Eventually the pain eased up and I gained some strength. I realized that I had some say in the outcome. Mindset is everything and it can cause one to succeed or fail. I wanted to succeed. I am honored that God chose me, and I beat stage 4 cancer. I vowed to impact society in a positive way for the rest of my days on this earth. I don't think it was dying that scared me. I couldn't bear the thought of just existing and not impacting society in some meaningful way. Whenever I am given the opportunity to speak, I make it very clear that being a single mom when I started my business is not my story; it's just a scene in my story. Being diagnosed with stage 4 cancer is not my story; it's just a scene in my story. I can't keep reliving the pain, disappointments or anger. I have to take responsibility for my part in it all and move on and live. I say when, I say how, and I say why. I am the author of my story and I get to write the outcome. No one can fill my cup or give me esteem. If it is to be, it is up to me.

Finally, wealthy people are vulnerable. Being vulnerable simply means one is open to receive. If you don't trust the mentors, coaches or leaders in your life then you have nothing coming. You have to allow your mentors to lead without hesitation. One reason many fail in this area is because they feel that everybody is out to get them, so the lack of trust holds them back. When the leader in your life has a vested interest, it only benefits them to lead you in the right direction. They will benefit as a result of your increase. Therefore, they will tell you everything you need to know to be successful because seeing you win allows them to win. Forgive those that have hurt you. Stop giving power to past disappointments. Forgiveness is more for your peace of mind than the one that caused the pain. You can forgive an individual for what they've done to you, but you don't have to let them back into your space. Once their fruit changes then you can consider whether you should fully open up or not. As a leader I make it very clear to my organization that if I don't know you, I can't lead you. Trust plays a great part in the success of your future. Once one goes through the stages listed above, they won't base their success on the opinions or approval of the naysayers because true wealth starts in their mind.

VISION

I've read many books in my lifetime and in my early years as an entrepreneur, like the contributing authors, I became a personal development fanatic. I knew that I had to change if ever I wanted to be somebody great. In looking back I realized that there are two types of readers: those that are interested in change and those that are committed to changing. When one is interested in something, they only implement the strategy when it's convenient. There's a saying, "Trying is just a noisy way of not doing something." Then there's the other type of reader that I strive to be daily, the Committed Reader. They execute the strategy no matter what. They don't use excuses.

The contributing authors in this book did an amazing job by sharing with you the key elements that moved their lives in multiple areas. How you do anything is how you do everything. The principles that they shared are principles that can be used in your Spiritual, Mental, Physical, Social/Relationships and Financial life. Allow the messages in these chapters to impact and move your life from bad to good or good to great. Use the principles to move you closer to the person you wish to become, from Vision to Reality.

We believe that true wealth starts in the mind. A made-up mind is a powerful weapon and it can tear down walls or it can build them up. You decide.

Thank you, authors, for all of your time and commitment to this project. I am forever honored and grateful to share this powerful weapon with you. A BOOK!! Let's continue to impact the world in our WALK, our TALK and our GIVING.

Much More Success to all of you.

Lisa M. Jones

A Message from Larry Weidel

AUTHOR OF *SERIAL WINNER*

It seems that everyone you talk to has their own personal idea of something great they'd like to do with their life, yet so few ever do. Of those who do wind up doing something great, most turn out to be one-time wonders—they find it hard to repeat their success. Yet, in spite of that, we all know people who seem to go through life from one success to another. They have the same setbacks we all do, yet somehow, they're able to minimize their disasters and maximize their successes. What makes them different? The answer is related to how they think and evaluate life, which starts with the facts and beliefs they base their thinking on. This forms the basis for their actions that create their success. Helping people make this mental breakthrough—that once your thinking starts to improve, your actions can start creating more success for you—was the basis of my bestselling book, *Serial Winner*, and probably the reason it resonated with so many who read it.

I took my cue from Art Williams, who said, "The world is full of people who almost do things. We need more people who do things." For lack of a better term, I call those people Serial Winners because they not only think of great things to do, but they're able to make them happen. When you look at the world, you find that it is dominated by these kinds of people—the kinds of people that do great things. They're the ones who are admired. They're the ones who are on TV, in the newspapers, and written about on the Internet. They become the heroes and role models for the next generation. They are the trendsetters, the style setters, the tone setters. They are the ones that sell out shows and fill football stadiums, basketball arenas, and concert halls. They dominate because they have had success and have become excellent at what they do. On the other hand, no one seems to be interested in the people who can never get anything done. But they're very interested in those that climb to the top . . . because that's what they want to do too.

When I was young, I was like everyone else—I had my own handful of interests that motivated me. I loved sports and competition. I loved creating, so I loved painting and photography. I didn't know how this would play out, but I did know those things motivated me more than other things. No one else in my family had any interest in those things, but I did . . . and that's all that mattered.

Along the way, I learned some important lessons that would shape my future. First, I made up my mind that I'd pay almost any price to be my own boss. Growing up, my father was in the military, so we moved every year. I wanted to be my own boss so no one could have the power to move me on a moment's notice. I also made up my mind that I'd do whatever it took to get to the top of whatever it was I was doing. I came to this conclusion after working menial summer jobs in high school. I clearly saw that not only did the people at the bottom make the least money, but they got the least respect. That was a lifestyle I didn't want. Living on an average income didn't seem to bother my parents or aunts and uncles much, but it sure bothered me. When I was in 6th grade, both my mother and my father had to take on part-time jobs. Even years later, when my father went to Vietnam for a year, my mother had to work as a cleaning woman to make ends meet. I knew I wasn't going to settle. There had to be a better way.

I did the only thing I could think to do: I followed my dreams and instincts. And I was fortunate enough to have many of these dreams come true . . . beyond my wildest expectations. Not only have I built a business all over North America in financial services that has paid me over $70 million dollars in career earnings, but I was also able to compete and excel in a lot of other different areas. Most recently, I now own an art gallery featuring my own paintings and photography in Palm Beach, FL. I also have photography and paintings hanging in Pergande Gallery and various venues all over Aspen, CO. And, to top it off, my book, *Serial Winner*, was named the #52 business book of all time in the success category

All of these accomplishments were beyond my wildest dreams. Today I still can't believe they all became reality, and of course, when I was a 17-year-old high school student, they would have been unimaginable. Starting out, I didn't know how my life would turn out—but I did know what motivated me, and I was driven to pursue those things.

Like I said in the beginning, most people have something great, maybe many great things, they want to do in their life, and they're looking for clues and answers. The great news is that successful patterns of thinking and acting can be learned. No one is born a winner—it's something you learn. I'm excited for you because you're getting ready to dive into this book, and it is full of information that can help you unlock the secrets that will let you become one of those people . . . the ones who do it, the ones who make their dreams come true.

Rene' L. Turner is committed to the mission of helping individuals "Develop Millionaire Minds". As the leader of The Millionaire Movement Team, Rene' has built a successful financial services business that impacts the under-served middle income market, one family at a time. She serves as a financial coach to her clients and a mentor to her many business partners.

Rene' earned a B.S. in Industrial and Systems Engineering from the Georgia Institute of Technology. She received the Young Engineering Alumnus Award and served on the Institute's Board of Trustees. She has been profiled in Essence magazine and Success From Home magazine.

Rene' has been married to Mel Turner for over 35 years and they have two daughters. René and Mel have been featured speakers at many Marriage Conferences during which they share strategies for having a "Real Marriage, God's Way".

RENE' L. TURNER

Sowing and Reaping

"Your mind is a garden; your thoughts are the seeds.
You can grow flowers or you can grow weeds."
Ritu Ghatourey

C hoices. I learned at an early age that life is about choices. I am
one of nine siblings. I have three older brothers and five younger
sisters. I have phenomenal, loving parents who have now been
married more than 60 years. My father pastored the same church for
thirty years and has been in the ministry for over 50 years. My mother
dedicated her life to not only raising her children but also nurturing
and educating hundreds of children at the church's school. My parents
believed that children should be trained and disciplined with love and
consistency. They made it very clear that actions had consequences. I
could choose to "act right" and be obedient and be rewarded with their
approval or "act out" and suffer the consequences. I decided early on
that the price of "acting out" was too embarrassing or painful to make
that choice very often. Now don't get it twisted; I learned through the
school of hard knocks that sighing too loudly, rolling my eyes, mutter-
ing under my breath, talking in church, and "forgetting" to wash the
dishes were choices that brought unwelcomed consequences.

One of the Bible verses that I remember my father preaching and teaching on frequently is,

> "Do not be deceived, God is not mocked;
> for whatever a man sows, that he will also reap."
> New King James Version, Galatians 6:7.

As you can see my lessons on Sowing and Reaping began early in my life. I grew up in an environment that emphasized academic success. My parents, relatives and teachers instilled in me the importance of doing my best in school. It was easy for me to see that choosing to do my homework and studying resulted in me excelling academically. I was a perennial honor student in high school who took the most advanced classes offered by my school and maintained a 4.0 GPA. I was willing to discipline my mind and my behavior in order to achieve my desired outcome of getting A's.

This trend continued when I went to college. I attended The Georgia Institute of Technology (Georgia Tech) and majored in Industrial Engineering. Georgia Tech is one of the most rigorous universities in this country and has world-renowned engineering and science programs. When I attended Freshman Orientation the Dean of Students said, "Look to your left and look to your right. One of you will not graduate from Georgia Tech." I looked to my left and right and smiled, but in my head, I thought, *I feel sorry for one of you because I am going to graduate.* Women and African Americans were under-represented at Tech and many professors barely hid their lack of belief in my ability to excel. Their lack of belief didn't bother me because I had developed a high level of belief in myself as a successful student. The curriculum was very difficult, and I experienced my first round of B's, C's and even one D in some classes. But I felt strongly that if I did the homework, studied and for the first time, ask for help,

I could excel. Once again, I experienced the confirmation of good choices bringing good consequences. I graduated with High Honors.

As a college freshman I made a decision to not only pursue academic success but to also stretch my wings as a leader. I quickly got involved in organizations that I believed in and poured my time and energy into helping those organizations achieve their missions and grow. I ultimately had membership and leadership roles in several prestigious organizations and honor societies, and I became the President of The Georgia Tech Society of Black Engineers. Sowing and Reaping, Sowing and Reaping…it really worked!

By now you must be thinking, "Girl, you had it going on in every area of your life." That is not correct. There was a void in my belief system in the area of Achieving Wealth. The congregation of my father's church was made up primarily of low income to low-middle income African American families. His salary was relatively small. My mother spent many years as a stay-at-home mom (no surprise considering she was raising nine children) and even when she worked as the Director of the church's school, she wasn't paid much money. Although we never lacked a meal or a roof over our heads, money was very tight. My mom cooked nearly every meal we ate, and she mastered recipes that could feed a lot of people on a small budget. We didn't wear "name-brand" fashion and most summer vacations consisted of time spent at my grandparents' house in Alabama. We would get excited to have a "fancy" Sunday dinner at Morrison's Cafeteria. There's no need to feel sorry for us because we were very happy. I actually thought we were middle-income until I attended integrated schools and I saw how real middle-income people lived.

Many seeds had been sown in my life regarding spiritual values, academic success and being a leader. Very few seeds had been sown regarding the potential for big financial success and becoming wealthy. There was a void in this area of my belief system.

When it comes to gardening, I have a very brown thumb. I am a plant murderer. But this is what I do know about a garden. Something is going to grow in a garden. If you have a garden meant for flowers but you don't plant any flowers, weeds will grow in place of the flowers. Even if you plant flowers, weeds will grow, but if you don't plant flowers all you will have is weeds. In the garden of your mind, weeds are negative thoughts and seeds are positive thoughts. You must be intentional and diligent to plant seeds and grow flowers, but weeds just grow with no effort or conscious thought. Since I didn't have many seeds or positive thoughts sown in my mind in relationship to wealth, I had a lot of weeds (negative thoughts) about money.

- Money is scarce
- Don't ask for or desire things that your family can't afford
- Wanting more means, you are greedy
- God only cares about my spiritual, mental and physical prosperity, not my financial prosperity
- Middle income status is all you should aspire to
- Be happy for what you have; lots of people have less than you

The section of the garden of my mind that dealt with financial prosperity was like an abandoned lot full of ugly weeds and sandspurs (if you grew up in Florida you know how painful it is to step on sandspurs). I had not applied the lessons of sowing and reaping in this area of my life.

After graduating from college and getting married to my phenomenal husband (and best friend) I was introduced to the company that I now have a successful business with and the concept of becoming financially independent and beyond that, even becoming wealthy. I met people who boldly declared their goals to help others and to build wealth for themselves and their families. I saw that most of the people I was meeting had the same spiritual and family values that I had, and they also had a belief that you could become wealthy and remain a great person. It was like the scales were falling from my eyes. I didn't have to choose between being a good person who served God or being wealthy. I could be BOTH!

I began to realize that I had not applied the same principles I used for academic success and being a successful leader of organizations and a successful employee to the area of financial success. I began to think about the fact that studying and working hard had served me well in all my other endeavors, so why wouldn't it also serve me well in the area of building wealth?

I realized that I needed to change my thinking so I could change my life. I began to read books and listen to audios on how to re-program your thinking. I began to put into practice the principles I was learning, and I began to grow in my understanding of the power of the mind and the fact that true wealth truly does start in the mind.

The first step is to plant the garden. You must start sowing the right seeds (positive thoughts). But even when you start sowing seeds in your flower garden, the garden has to be tended. It's so easy for weeds (negative thoughts) to slip in and choke out the flowers.

PLANTING THE GARDEN

I had to change my beliefs in order to change my thoughts. I had to change my thoughts in order to change my words. I had to change my words in order to change my behavior.

BELIEFS

I had to learn to trust God's call on my life. As I began to build my financial services business, I became confident that I had found God's will for my life. After starting the business part-time, I left my engineering career and became a full-time entrepreneur. I know that my financial services business is my ministry. God did not call me to be a missionary or to serve in a role that paid a low income. He called me to be a business builder in the financial services space. If I excelled in this arena, a high income and the ability to gain wealth were the expected outcomes. The more value I deliver, the more financial success I will have. The more financial success I have, I am more able to bless those who were called, like my parents, to ministries that didn't provide a high income.

Whenever I find myself struggling with doubt and a lack of belief in what God can do in and through and for me, I think of the scripture in Mark 9:23-24 (NIV).

"If you can?" said Jesus. "Everything is possible for one who believes." Immediately the boy's father exclaimed, "I do believe; help me overcome my unbelief!"

That is my prayer – "Lord, help me overcome my unbelief."

THOUGHTS

As I began to study more about the power of the mind, I realized that I had to learn to unleash the power of my thoughts in a positive way instead of a negative way. I had to replace my limiting beliefs and thoughts about money with empowering beliefs and thoughts.

I realized that I had to "think about" what I was "thinking about." I began to notice that I often emotionalized my negative thoughts about money. I would think about an undesirable financial situation that I might be facing and unleash emotions of worry and fear about the situation. This was like applying fertilizer to weeds. The more I thought about my negative circumstances with strong emotions, the more negative thoughts I had. I was literally choking out the positive thoughts. As I became more aware of my thoughts, I was able to recognize the negative thoughts and emotions faster. I could then proactively "pull them out" and replace them with positive thoughts and emotions of hope regarding the situations and circumstances that I desired financially. These positive thoughts and emotions attracted additional empowering and positive thoughts and emotions. I learned to replace

- "I don't ever have enough money" with "money is abundant in my life"
- "I can't ever get ahead" with "great things always happen to me"
- "Nothing is going my way" with "I attract people and money"

WORDS

I learned that it wasn't enough to "think" about the life I wanted; I had to "speak" about it. I had to have the courage to talk about the life I wanted. I had to talk about it not only to myself, but I also had to have the courage to talk about it even among people who might not agree with me. I even named my business team "The Millionaire Movement" so it would be apparent to everyone that becoming a millionaire and helping others do the same is the mission of my business. I have to unleash the power of my words every day. The only voice I hear 24 hours a day, 365 days a year is my own, so I must say the right things to myself, about myself and my ability to create wealth.

BEHAVIOR

I recognized that I must have a desire to Be More and a willingness to Do More in order to Have More. Wealthy people have a profit motive. My goal in business is to provide great service to my clients and my team and help them achieve their goals. My goal to make a profit in my business is just as important. My two daughters were young when I began building my business. Although I made it a priority to spend meaningful time with them, I also had to be away from them a lot in order to develop and grow my business. It was very important to me that I didn't waste the time that I was away from them by doing things that didn't make me money in the short term or long term. My attitude was, "If I am going to be away from my babies while I meet with this potential client or business partner, my intention better be to close business or expand my team." Needless to say, I wasn't successful on every appointment, but my goal was to make every appointment profitable. I had no interest in just being busy, I needed to get results.

TENDING THE GARDEN

Now that you have planted the garden you have to work just as hard to tend it by keeping the weeds out.

- Be careful about who you allow to influence you. You can like someone without allowing them to influence your choices. Be deliberate about finding people you admire not just because of their financial success but also because of their values, lifestyle and the example they set.

- Develop Daily Disciplines that will help you nurture the seeds you planted. I make it a priority to have a daily Quiet Time where I read the Bible and pray. Having a time to meditate and seek direction is very important. You should also work on self-improvement every day. Read or listen to a chapter of a book. Write down your goals and read your affirmations. These disciplines will help you dominate the day.

- Be conscious of your thoughts so you can identify the weeds (negative thoughts) and pull them out. Make sure you replace them with more seeds (positive thoughts).

- Dream of expanding your garden. An unlimited God gives us permission to have unlimited dreams. It doesn't take any more effort to dream big than it does to think small. Dreaming big doesn't cost you any money. Visualize your dream by making a Vision Board. Touch your dreams by touring a house similar to your dream house and test driving your dream car.

 I have learned that every time I achieve a goal or a dream it is vital that I replace it with a bigger goal or dream. When I fail to do that, I become stagnant and am more willing to accept the status quo. The bottom line is if you are still living, you should still be dreaming.

- Ignore the naysayers. There will always be people who want to tell you that your pursuit of wealth is misplaced.

- They say "money won't buy you happiness."

- I say "money may not buy me happiness, but it will sure calm my nerves while I look for happiness."

- They say "money isn't the most important thing in the world." I say "taking care of everyone that's important to me costs money."

- They say "you are working too hard; you need to slow down."

- I say "I will be able to rest all I want once I hit my goal."

REAPING THE HARVEST

As you can see, sowing the right seeds and removing the weeds requires you to be consistent, disciplined, focused and diligent. You can't opt out of the work. If you visit your local florist or farmer's market and see bin after bin of beautiful flowers, you should be mindful of the fact that lots of effort was invested in order to achieve the bountiful harvest. All of that hard work was invested to grow flowers that will have a fairly short life.

The great news is when you invest the hard work to cultivate the garden of your mind, the harvest of wealth that you reap can impact you, your family and your community. The creation of wealth has the capacity to change the next generation. The full harvest doesn't appear overnight, or even in one "growing" season. The joy comes from day after day fighting the battle for controlling your mind, planting positive thoughts and yanking out negative thoughts. You gain satisfaction from setting a goal and achieving it and then setting another goal and achieving it, over and over again. As your reality comes more and more into alignment with your dreams it encourages you to keep fighting the good fight.

I believe the creation of wealth is a journey, not a destination. The person you become on the journey is just as important as the realization of the goal. I have had to make so many changes in myself up to this point in my journey. Although many of the changes were difficult, they were all changes I needed to make in order to become the person God created me to be. I have a multitude of goals I still want to achieve, and I know I will have to continue to grow in order to achieve them. I will be sowing seeds of positive thoughts and pulling out weeds of negative thoughts all along the way to my harvest. I will do it with sweat on my brow and a song in my heart and gratitude to God for giving me another day to create the life of my dreams.

 **Collis Temple III,** owns and operates Collis Temple III & Associates, a Training Center with over 550 licensed agents. Prior to pursuing his own dreams of business ownership, Collis was a student-athlete playing basketball at Louisiana State University. While at LSU he earned an undergraduate Degree in General Business in three years. He then completed a Masters in Sports Management, before beginning the pursuit of his Doctorate in Educational Leadership. According to LSU's Sports Information Department, Collis is believed to be the first Division I student athlete to complete an undergraduate degree, Master's degree, and began the pursuit of a Doctorate while still eligible to play athletics. In January 2015 Collis was appointed by the Governor to the Louisiana Board of Regents, the highest decision-making board of Higher Education in the State of LA. In January 2019, Collis was voted Vice-Chairman of the Board.

Collis also serves the community by serving on the Board of Directors of the Knock Knock Children's Museum in Baton Rouge, as well as the 100 Black Men of Metro Baton Rouge.

In 2016 Collis published his first book, Work Like a Slave, Think Like a Master.

Collis is the husband of Britney Temple and father to three amazing children – Monet (8), Eden (6), Collis IV (4). Collis' mantra in business is FINANCIAL LITERACY = ECONOMIC EMPOWERMENT = REAL CHANGE in OUR COMMUNITIES!

COLLIS TEMPLE III

Respect the Process

R espect – (verb) to hold in esteem or honor
Process – (noun) a systematic series of actions directed to
some end

To Respect the Process means to hold in high esteem or honor the systematic series of actions directed to some end. That "end" could mean a lot of things. In the case of this chapter, that "end" has to do with YOUR SUCCESS. When you hold something in high esteem or honor something, that means you approach it with reverence and not haphazardly. It means that you give every area careful consideration because you truly recognize that it isn't an overnight evolution. When it comes to understanding the systematic series of actions directed to some end, in terms of "the process," you clearly realize that there are several pieces that go into you accomplishing what it is you've set out to do. When you put both of these together, you understand, accept, and maximize your success, you quickly embrace, Respect for the Process! When you truly Respect the Process then YOUR SUCCESS is INEVITABLE! What better set of words in the same sentence could there be than "Your Success" and "Inevitable?"

In reference to Respecting the Process, let's take the process of pregnancy. A normal pregnancy usually lasts about 40 weeks and it's a pretty complicated process. Every week during the process serves a purpose and when a child is born prematurely, they aren't allowed to go home right away because they haven't completed the process of growth, therefore they stay in the NICU (Neonatal Intensive Care Unit). A person would never expect that a baby born after 28 weeks should be able to function like a baby who has gone full-term without having spent time in the NICU, gotten strong, and at least come very close to completing the process of growth as a newborn. Let us consider the gestational process of the elephant, for example. The elephant has the longest gestational period of any other mammal on the planet. The Asian elephant is pregnant for 18 – 22 months, while the African Bush elephant is pregnant for 22 months. Think about that, ladies—22 months pregnant? Some of you probably want to close the book at this point!! The reality of that situation though is that you want to go FULL TERM to make sure that the baby elephant comes out fully formed and ready to conquer the world. That's the same way that things are when it comes to our GOALS and DREAMS!

Why then would anyone expect their GOALS and DREAMS to come to pass without completing whatever specific process they have to complete to accomplish the things that they would like and see their aspirations become REALITY? Ask yourself that: Why abort your goals and dreams without allowing them to go FULL TERM?

Remember that you don't want to treat your destiny like a TV dinner; you better use the crock pot. Don't try to microwave a miracle. There's always a process involved. The reality for most of us, if we were to buckle down, learn the process, accept the process, and jump wholeheartedly into applying and putting the process to work for us, is we could actually speed our process up! Unlike pregnancy, which always takes 40 weeks, we can COLLAPSE TIME FRAMES when it comes to our success based on the work that we put in. Remember, collapsing time frames and cutting corners are two totally different things! When I speak of collapsing time frames let's use, for example, a sales associate that has a goal of hitting certain numbers in a defined period of time. That person must RESPECT THE PROCESS that it'll take to create the success that they want. That process more than likely will include and involve initial prospecting for potential clients or new associates, making the necessary number of phone calls based on ratios and numbers, perfecting their presentation once they get the opportunity to get in front of those potentials, and closing. There are numbers involved that they cannot get around. They cannot expect that they can recruit five people or close five sales based on five appointments. That's not how the PROCESS works. There may be the few opportunities when they go five for five, but that's not the norm and they have to UNDERSTAND and ACCEPT that and WORK those numbers accordingly.

I'm a HUGE fan of the idea of the THREE COMMON DENOMINATORS for SUCCESS, and those three common denominators apply perfectly to the idea of RESPECTING THE PROCESS.

The Three Common Denominators for all Successes are as follows:

1) Coachability
2) Focus
3) Work Ethic

COACHABILITY

I would define the first of the common denominators as the ability to seek out, accept, internalize, and apply information that is given by someone who may be a mentor or expert in the area you're looking to excel in. This applies directly to respecting the process because you won't be clear on what the process truly looks like without having some type of mentor who has either done it or at least is in the process of doing it. What you need to be clear on is, that mentor may or MAY NOT be a PERSONAL mentor. That person may or MAY NOT even be alive. You can gain information and knowledge from books, audios, podcasts, and a host of other self-improvement materials. Don't get me wrong; it's always better to have someone who's done it that you can go back and forth with and get questions answered but getting the knowledge versus not getting the knowledge is always the best!

When it comes to COACHABILITY, there are three parts: 1) Seeking out the Coaching, 2) Accepting and Internalizing that Coaching, 3) Doing that and then some. As it relates to respecting the process you've got to first do as mentioned earlier by seeking out the mentorship, wherever it may be found – in person, through a third party, etc. Next it's about Accepting and Internalizing that coaching and respecting that you aren't better than the ratios or the numbers, or that somehow you will be immune to the process. This is something that often catches people off guard, especially those who have experienced success in other fields or consider themselves to be very talented. This is a major part of RESPECTING THE PROCESS. Third, it comes down to doing that and then some and ACTION SUPERSEDES everything! That's what respecting the process is all about – DOING what's necessary to achieve the goals and dreams you have and making them a reality! Remember, you don't have to reinvent the wheel; plagiarize your way to success by being coachable!

FOCUS

Focus is defined as the ability to stay locked in on a goal or dream regardless of life happening around you. This is obviously a critical part of RESPECTING THE PROCESS because this is what really runs most people away from their success – often, more than the actual work. A person's success many times comes down to their ability to block out the inevitable life occurrences that will come to pass, regardless of the seriousness or triviality of those situations. If Coachability plays a role in gaining clarity about what it takes to succeed, FOCUS in relation to setting goals and locking in on those goals, along with the process that goes with that, is also of paramount importance. It's extremely hard to hit a goal you haven't set.

Writing your goals and affirmations is also a critical piece of the process in terms of your focus because the process strengthens your resolve to make your goals a reality. Your conscious mind is looking to validate your beliefs, so improving and, in some cases, changing those beliefs is a crucial part of the process.

WORK ETHIC

The definition of work ethic is "a belief in the moral benefit and importance of work and its inherent ability to strengthen character." One of my favorite scriptures is 2 Thessalonians 3:10 (NIV), which says, "The one who is unwilling to work shall not eat." Without application of what you were coachable to get and learn and the game plan that you were focused on laying out and carefully constructing the how-tos and what-tos for – there exists NO SUCCESS.

Taking the action above and beyond everything else is what RESPECTING THE PROCESS is all about. If you truly respected the process and wanted the spoils of what that legitimate respect would yield, you'd be practicing the necessary actions that would lead to complete goal accomplishment! That can be a tough pill to swallow but it's true. In terms of success, EFFORT many times is the great EQUALIZER as well as the great SEPARATOR!

To truly put yourself in the mental place where you can maximize your success and respect the process at a level that most people would find amazing (because most people are average), you've legitimately got to redefine what COMFORT is for you. Think about it: You're not FAILING at anything that you're COMFORTABLE at. You've got to realize something you undoubtedly have heard before, "Your success has nothing to do with how you feel!" Ask yourself, "What feelings do I feed?" At the end of the day, EVERYTHING'S HARD before it's EASY. Pick your HARD based on the respect you give to the process. You can deal with a few no's through the process in order to achieve amazing levels of success, or you can deal with the hard of not having, and even tougher, knowing you had an opportunity to do it but didn't, and even worse than that, having those around you who actually took the actions that you weren't willing to take and are achieving amazing levels of success!

Though I am grateful

for the blessings of wealth,

it hasn't changed who I am.

My feet are still on the ground.

I'm just wearing better shoes.

OPRAH WINFREY

Joseph Ward is a Senior National Sales Director at one of the largest financial services companies in North America. He has 23 years of experience in the financial services industry specializing in Life Insurance & Investments.

Joseph has numerous certifications including his Life insurance license, and his series 6, 63 and 26 Investment licenses. His organization consists of numerous Regional Vice Presidents that operate 23 branch offices in the Chicagoland area with 850 agents. He's received numerous industry and company awards and is a highly sought after International Public Speaker.

JOE WARD

Manifesting Money

The beginning of my story may not be too different than yours. Growing up, I was not surrounded by wealthy people, nor was my family from money. I did not have the educational background or come from a school system that taught anything about financial principles, money or wealth. At first glance, my background is not one that would seem to lead to money or the accumulation of wealth, but here is where my path takes a turn for the better. About 23 years ago, I made one of the best decisions of my life and entered the financial services arena, deciding at that moment that my past would not dictate my future.

What I've learned over the last 23 years is that the manifestation of wealth starts in one's mind. Working in the financial services field, I not only learned the principles of money, but I learned the mental side of it. I was taught the correlation between the informational and operational side of money, but then there is the thought process behind money. It is what I call, Manifesting Money.

The first thing that I want to reference is a very universal thought process, not an original thought but a universal concept that Thoughts are Things. Most people believe that there is something that you must do to generate and accumulate money. This is only partially true. In addition to the operational things that you've got to put in place, there are things that must happen on a day-to-day basis in the psyche of your mind. All material wealth and monetary possessions, as Napoleon Hill, author of *Think and Grow Rich*, states, begin in the mind.

Our minds exist on a conscious and a subconscious level. The conscious level is where awareness occurs. The conscious mind includes such things as the sensations, perceptions, memories, feelings, and fantasies inside our current awareness. Conversely, things that the conscious mind wants to keep hidden from awareness are repressed into the subconscious mind. But the good news is that we can directly and deliberately change our subconscious mind. The subconscious mind does not know the difference between what is real and what is not real; it only knows the thoughts that are planted in it. Each thought is a seed and each seed carry power. The thoughts will eventually manifest into our physical world, and that is what is meant by thoughts are things. Therefore, everything, when it comes to the creation of wealth, begins with a thought.

Our actual brain or mind works just like a GPS. Most people today use that technology within their phones. First, you must decide where it is you want to go, but the destination must be specific, not ambiguous. What do I mean by that? I mean that it would be very unclear to say you want to go to the West Coast, for example. Telling the GPS, your destination is the West Coast is very ambiguous. It is an undefined goal/game plan. Now you could start heading in that direction but you're going to probably end up in Kansas, or maybe even Florida. But if you know specifically where you want to go, let's say, Los Angeles, California, then all you must do is put that destination into the GPS and the GPS will guide you there.

LOST

The first mistake people make when it comes to accumulating wealth and money is that most people don't know the destination. They don't know where they want to go. They are ambiguous in the thoughts that are placed in their subconscious mind, like: *I want to be rich; I want to be wealthy, I want financial independence, etc. ...* They do not give it a specific destination and therefore they never reach it. They are simply headed to the West Coast of wealth accumulation, which is an ambiguous location which can never be reached.

RECALCULATING

Using the example of Los Angeles, California, once the destination was put into the GPS then arrival at that destination is certain UNLESS you change your mind and give it another instruction. If I program the GPS to go to Los Angeles and I'm headed down that road and decide, "You know what? I don't want to go to Los Angeles anymore, now I want to go to Texas," it will continue to guide you to Los Angeles unless you reprogram it to go to Texas. You've given the GPS a specific instruction, but once you give it a different instruction, it will guide you to a different destination. Our internal GPS works on the same principle, except our words and thoughts are the programming.

If I say I want to be a millionaire or a cash millionaire, I have put an instruction inside the GPS of my mind, and I will start a journey to go there. The power is in stating your desire in a clear and concise manner. People state this desire daily as they play the lottery, Powerball and Mega Millions. You may have even stated that desire while reading this book and may be saying to yourself, "Well then why doesn't everybody become a millionaire?" Simple, because they put in a different instruction and they counteract the first instruction. They cause their mind to recalculate and head in a different direction. The thoughts that are now being deposited in the mind are thoughts like: *Nobody in my family has ever been a millionaire, I don't come from a background of money* (that was my thought), or *no one in my family has ever generated any amount of wealth, I can't be a millionaire.* The GPS of the mind is now on another course. It is headed to Texas, instead of Los Angeles. It will never reach the destination of millionaire. What you input will always control what you output.

The key is controlling the input. In order to have the desired results, our thoughts must be specifically directed toward our desired outcome. They must be continuous, correct thoughts that point in the direction of wealth creation. The thoughts must be definitive. Your destination must be an exact amount of money because the mind cannot process abstract thoughts like wealth, financial freedom, financial independence or rich. These terms are relative and mean different things to different people. But definitive terms such as a $1,000,000 a year or $83,334 a month are thoughts that the mind can decipher and digest. The great thing is that this works in all areas of our lives. For example, if you're seeking a positive relationship or if you desire to be healthy; it is the same process. Whatever you focus on grows. It is our consciously concentrated thoughts that will manifest in our lives.

Thoughts about wealth must be intentional. There must be an exact plan, there must be an exact thought process, there must be an exact period and there must be an exact method to attain wealth. The level of intention will bring about the speed at which money is accumulated, or, more importantly, attracted. The more specific we are, the more our mind manifests that intended result.

Many times, this may be thought about from a religious standpoint, but it's also thought about in the secular world. The source of what's going to end up happening is still the same in your mind. If you believe in spiritual things, if you believe in God like I do, then you believe that God is going to give you the power within your mind to impact and influence the manifestation. If you don't believe in a higher power (and there are a percentage of people in the world that don't believe in God), if you don't believe in a greater power then the source is still your mind in terms of that manifestation. Therefore, the clearer that you are, the more specific you are, the more outlined you are in your approach, the speedier the actual manifestation.

The universe (which is not specific to what your religious beliefs are) only understands specificity. The universe only understands clarity. If you are clear, then the universe is clear. If you are fuzzy or confused, doubtful or fearful—if you are all those things then the universe will be in alignment with who you are. Again, if I don't have an actual direction, anywhere I end up is good. Another great example would be, "I want to be a millionaire." But even with that you must be careful with the instruction because you may be limiting what your capacity is to manifest. But you must start somewhere that is realistic to yourself.

Understanding time frames is key. Once you have given an instruction to your mind that you are specific about, how long will it take to manifest? According to the principle of seed, time and harvest, in the spiritual world the universe must manifest your instruction (the seed) if you don't change your mind. What is confusing to people is time frame, because the universe in no way, shape or form has ever guaranteed a time frame, meaning if you ask for this right now you will get it. Nowhere in the Bible or the Koran or even the works of Buddha is that stated. You may request it, you may make an earnest request, but there is nowhere within any of those references that says, "It will be done when you say it." There will be times when that does happen, but that is not a guarantee, nor a prerequisite. Your job is to make a request. The scriptures would call that a petition; you make a petition to the Father and then it's either going be honored now or it will be honored in the time frame of the universe. But it is going to happen!

Another key is trusting God. Once you make the petition to God, you must now believe that God is going to honor it if you don't change your mind. Sometimes there is a test to see how serious you are, how committed you are and how strong your faith is in that request. Most people's minds are doubtful about the fact that money can come into their possession based on their thought process. What you must understand is there is no shortage of money in the world. There is no quota in terms of the number of people that can become wealthy.

I heard it once stated in a seminar that I attended that money is just like currency. Money is also called currency. It is called currency because it operates like electricity, which is something that flows. Electricity is constantly flowing. Now here's the key: Whether you access it or not, that electricity is flowing.

If you're at your home and there is an outlet there, and you want to charge your cell phone, the electricity is already flowing through that outlet. You are utilizing it the moment that you take your cell phone and connect it to that outlet. If that's the case, then we can see the same example that there is no shortage of money. The money is available; it is already flowing. What have you plugged into that source to be able to utilize and receive the flow of money?

If money is like currency and it is flowing continuously, then it is much like the flow of water. If we go to a faucet or we go to a shower, there is a reservoir of water that is already available. It is simply waiting for you. You must be the one that gives the instruction by turning the faucet. You give the instruction that you are now ready for that water to release from the reservoir. But you must believe that the water is already there. When we go in to brush our teeth in the morning, we're not questioning the fact that we've turned that faucet on and water's going to come out. That water is going to come out based on our belief system and faith. We have to have the same type of belief system when it comes to money. We must say to ourselves, "All I have to do is turn on the faucet of money and money will eventually flow to me. And it will be endless, based on my belief system." That's the key. Whether it's electricity or whether it's water, you must control the flow. To what capacity do you control the flow? You control the flow based on your belief and based on your faith.

I always say, most people do not have a money consciousness; most people have a poverty mentality or a shortage type of thought process. We don't have the thought process that overflow is available. That's something that is discussed in the religious community, a spirit of overflow, but most of the time it's just lip service. It's things that we say because they are trendy or cliché.

I tell people that wanting money is not enough. It is not enough to say, "I wanna be wealthy." Everybody wants to be wealthy. Everybody has hopes and wishes and dreams but that is not enough. You must understand that whether or not that money is accumulated, whether it is attracted to you, whether or not it is manifesting in your life is a decision that you are making about, first of all, the presence of money, the availability of it, and that there is a method, an actual method, an actual game plan that we have discussed at least in part, on how to get there. There is a capacity that you have emotionally that will turn that faucet on; it will turn that electrical outlet on. It is the passion that you have, the level of intensity that you have, that this is something that you want in your life. It is something that is a requirement within your life for you to live the type of lifestyle that you want to live. But not only that, it's your birthright.

Psalm 24:1 starts with "the earth is the Lord's and the fullness thereof, the world, and they that dwell therein." If God owns it all and desires for His children to attain wealth (Deuteronomy 8:18), why are you broke? That's a question that you must ask yourself. You can't just be enthusiastic about it; you have to be passionate about it and you have to be consistent with that passion.

Again, why are you broke? I believe it's because too often we have heard that money is the root of all evil when in fact the scripture says, the *love* of money is the root of all evil. But when someone hears over and over that money is the root of all evil then one believes the lies like: you don't need all this money, money is bad, why would anyone need all this money, and it becomes a reflection about how one truly feels about money and blocks all instructions toward wealth.

There is a way that you feel about money. There's a thought process that you currently have about what money is and the purpose of it. Is it good? Is it bad? Is it for good people or evil people? The first thing you must accept is that money is an inanimate object. Money is neither good nor bad. It is a form of currency, a mode of exchanging compensation for goods or services. However, whether it is used for good or bad is determined by the hands of the person who possesses it.

This key is important to understand because you can do everything that I've discussed:

- you can make up your mind about it,
- you can get emotional about it,

- you can have a time frame,
- you can be specific, and
- you can tap into the power source

And money will still not manifest in your life. The reason this happens is because of the way you feel about it.

How do you feel about money? Is it something that you do not feel good about? If so, in order to manifest money, you are going to have to change your perspective on money. Again, money is an inanimate object. It is not alive. Its sole purpose is for use. How you decide to use money is the key. You must begin to feel good about how money will translate positively in your life. What are some positive things that you would be able to do for your significant other, your children, your church, your overall community; if you simply had the money to do it? But if you are looking at money in a negative way, you are actually pushing it away.

When you change your consciousness that this inanimate object in the hands of someone like yourself is going to be able to create a greater good in your overall community, in your overall world, and specifically in your own household, coupled with a positive feeling about money and utilizing the other key components discussed in this chapter, money must MANIFEST and come to you!

Money desires a home. I consistently share that money has an anthropomorphic (the attribution of human traits, emotions or intentions to a non-human entity) aspect to it. Money wants a place to stay where it is going to be cared for, grown, and multiplied. Money does not want to be in a place that is a negative environment. You find that if money is attracted to you in a small stream and you squander it, you will have a different mentality about it. You will have a different thought process about it that's not positive in nature, that's not conducive in nature to growth. Consequently, it's going to find another place to live where the environment is one of growth, overflow and positivity—a place where it feels cared for, grows and multiplies.

In conclusion, to manifest money, what must I do? What are my actions steps?

1. WHAT: The first thing is you must know exactly what it is that you want. I can tell you that is in reference to your own consciousness, that's in reference to your own heart, that's in reference to your own belief system; it is in reference to the size of the mission that you have, what you believe you were put on this planet to accomplish. Once you figure out what that mission is, the spirit or the universe is going to let you know how much money is needed for you to accomplish that. It starts with your own household, though. It starts with your own generation.

2. WHEN: Once you know what you want, figure out when specifically, you want that to happen. That means an actual date. That date is not promised but you've got to have that date. It must be realistic; it must be elastically realistic. You can't say you're going to be a millionaire next weekend. That doesn't make any sense; first of all, you don't personally believe it. But could you do that in five years based on your level of faith and belief? Yes. Could you do it in 10 years? Most definitely. Could you do it in 30 years? Well, that should be everybody.

3. WHY: Now that you know exactly what you want, now you know exactly when you want it, we've already talked about, deep in your consciousness, why? There has to be a reason you're doing it. It can't just be, "I want money," because that would be money

without an assignment and all money must have an assignment if you're going to keep it. Every dollar you have needs to have a name on it, meaning there is a purpose for it. Money without purpose goes away quickly. It runs away from you. What is your reason why? Why do you want money? It should start with your family, then maybe your church or your community and then the world!

The biggest part that keeps most people from being able to accomplish what we're talking about is they just don't know what they're willing to give to get it. There is no increase without sacrifice. It is called seed time and harvest time. It is called sowing and reaping. There is no accumulation of wealth where you have given nothing in exchange; you must give an idea, and you're going to give a tremendous amount of your time, your energy. You are going to sacrifice some of your schedule. You're going to sacrifice maybe some family time, maybe some time at your religious events. There must be an exchange of time and money that must then lead to the manifestation of the money you want to see come into your life.

The manifestation of your desired cash flow is only limited by your understanding and application of these principles.

 **Dr. Tasheka L. Green**, servant leader, educator, inspirational speaker, transformational coach, six-time author, entrepreneur, philanthropist, and talk show host, is the Founder, President, and Chief Executive Officer of To Everything There is a Season, Inc. Her innovative coaching techniques influence personal, professional development and organizational change. She leads with a focus to support individuals and organizations in identifying their purpose. Dr. Green's work garnered her a feature in the Harvard University School of Education, HarvardX Course, Introduction to Data Wise: A Collaborative Process to Improve Learning & Teaching.

A scholarly and virtuous woman, her extraordinary faith, vision, talents, presence, and accomplishments have allowed her to obtain a plethora of recognitions and awards. Dr. Green is an example of when preparation meets opportunity, the end result is success. She loves God and radiates with the joy of the Lord.

Dr. Green is married to William Z. Green, Sr., and they have three beautiful children, Marquis (21), Mikayla (8), and William Jr. (6).

DR. TASHEKA L. GREEN

Stretching the Elasticity of Your Mind...Focus on the Promise and Not the Moment

True Wealth Starts in the Mind: Whatever a man sets his mind to will not be denied, is a level-up call, for me, you, us, to stretch the elasticity of our mind beyond the present by looking toward the future. This call meant that I had to obtain a futuristic growth mindset, with a focus on how do I get better, rather than how am I doing. Before taking on a futuristic growth mindset, when people would ask, "How are you doing?" My response would be, "I am doing well." I always responded well, because deep within, I knew if I really told them how I was doing, they could not handle my truth. Also, I did not want to spend time explaining how I was doing if they did not have the answer I needed. So I would hide behind my smile and reply, "I am doing well." However, within me, it seemed like life had thrown me lemons and I couldn't even get enough juice out of them to make lemonade.

If I was thinking I was broke, then it manifested never having enough money. If I was thinking I would never be successful, then it manifested unsuccess. If I was thinking, if it isn't one thing it's another, then right around the corner was one more thing. I had mastered living paycheck to Monday and knew what it took to get through the next two weeks. I got comfortable with my life, settled in my own complacency, and allowed this to silence the parts of my mind that ignited change. At this point, I realized that my life was reflecting what my mind was thinking and not the intended plan of God: to prosper me, bring me hope, and a future. I had to renew my mind so that my entire life could be whole. I did not just want to be healed from being broke; rather, I desired to be liberated from the bondage of brokenness. I wanted no lack in every area of my life. I wanted to experience the fullness and the fruitfulness of wealth—physically, mentally, emotionally, financially, and spiritually. I wanted a harvest, and not just a harvest—I wanted it to replenish and multiply.

I was the leading role of my own show, an encore performance of a daily running mental monologue between my conscious and unconscious beliefs. One side of me was dancing with brokenness, but another side of me was singing songs of a place called better. I knew better was near, but I just could not seem to get there. Is this what it meant to be double-minded? Was I unstable? And if I was unstable, did that mean all my ways were unbalanced? When I would think positively, my bank account reminded me of something differently. I was thinking in the box and didn't even have enough courage to at least take the lid off and try to get out. That wealthy, better place, just seemed so distant, it was going to take a whole journey to get there, and I had already started late. In my mind, I was dividing myself from what was intended for my life by playing seesaw with the present and the future. My mind was interfering with the place God wanted me to be.

The instability and surrendering to brokenness not only impacted me financially; it impacted every area of my life. What I thought I had mastered began to overtake me. The hardship turned into financial struggles in the form of filing Chapter 20 (Chapter 7 and 13) bankruptcy. In my marriage, I contemplated committing adultery and pursuing a divorce. I stood in food pantry lines awaiting food for my family. We were nestled in our home during the winter months without heat and the summer months without air conditioning. I was teaching my children how to tell lies, by telling them the lights were off because there was a power outage in our neighborhood.

I recycled plastic jugs and filled them up with coins to take them to the grocery store, late at night, to exchange for cash. I drove the car on empty, because I knew exactly how much gas I had left before it would stop. The home of my mind was invaded with anxiousness, unhappiness, and doubt. Anxiousness was my bed, unhappiness was my pillow, and doubt was my blanket. I had no wants, no desires, no dreams, only one cry of help for my needs. As I reflect over where I was, where I am and what I am becoming, the only thing that had me bound was my pride and my mind. I could have been free and released from where I was earlier if I had dropped my pride and changed my mind. I was engulfed in my pride and swallowed up in my thoughts. If I had just stretched the elasticity of my mind and focused on the promise and not the moment, my situation could have been better. I had to train my mind to think in a place called better, abundance, overflow, more than enough. I had to eliminate all of the doubt, negative thoughts, the self-fulfilling prophecies, and reply to them with thoughts of faith, positivity, and affirmations. I had to pull myself up by my own bootstraps and say with confidence and power, "Enough is enough!"

I had to change and be transformed by renewing my mind. I had to have a laser focus and not be deceived by others' perceptions of success. So often, we are deceived by what we see, because so many people are living out their fantasies rather than their reality. Then we get drawn to this and have a perception that success is a person, place or thing. Then in return, we measure success by money, power, fame or position. Dr. Maya Angelou said, "Success is liking yourself, liking what you do, and liking how you do it." When I looked at myself, my life, my situation, I did not like what I saw, nor did I like what it was producing. I had settled in my mind and accepted broke. I had deactivated my faith, forfeited my inheritance, and was in a state of lack of complete satisfaction. This is when I shifted my mind and renounced broke, dismissed struggle, and said farewell to hardship. I began to create the conditions of wealth by renewing my mind, transforming my thoughts, speaking words of wisdom, and activating my actions. I had nothing to lose, but everything to gain. In summary, I stopped settling for less than my birthright and began walking in my inheritance.

I had to sort out the priorities in my life, declutter the compartments of my mind, release from needing success, and align my life back to the plan of God. In this moment I had a "mind spurt." I mentally matured in my mind. Just like being broke was a choice, wealth is a choice. Just like poverty was a choice, prosperity is a choice. Just like broke was a choice, being whole is a choice. I had options, and I had to choose if I wanted the former or the latter. So I chose wealth, prosperity, and being whole. The real change started in my mind, and manifested in every area in my life. My intrinsic motivation to become better was my daily driver, never stopping when I was tired, but rather when I reached a place called completion.

Are you ready to stretch the elasticity of your mind by looking toward the future and not the moment? Are you ready to renounce your plans and walk in your birthright and inheritance? Are you ready to think yourself wealthy, prosperous and whole? If you are, then take heed to these four key principles that will help you to get your mind back, take hold of your life, and walk in a wealthy, prosperous, and whole manner.

PRINCIPLE 1
CHANGE YOUR MINDSET

Do not conform to this world but be transformed by renewing your mind. You will never conquer your mind if you do not own where you are, overcome the challenges in your life, and acknowledge that "real" change is needed. You cannot take your old mindset into the new places you are going and are becoming. Assess your thinking, adjust your mind, and think like you have never thought before. Your mindset will determine your action, which will determine your outcome. When you change your mind, you will change your entire life.

PRINCIPLE 2
ALIGN YOUR MIND

We have many plans for our life, but only the purpose of God will prevail. The intended plan for you is to prosper you, to bring you hope and a future. A mental realignment is the maintenance that is needed to align your thoughts to the thoughts of God. You were born to be a success. You were born to be a winner. Anything other than that is not the path intended for you. So make the shift and align your thoughts back to what you were born to do and become.

PRINCIPLE 3
STABILIZE YOUR MIND

Stabilize your mind by owning your truth, letting go of your pride, renouncing your thoughts, and setting yourself totally free. Eliminate all the noise and distractions and be clear about the sound that is speaking to you. When you are stable you are strong, secure, firm, fastened, and in a position to receive and maintain what you receive. Stabilizing your mind allows you to be a good steward over what you have been given and responsible for what you have been entrusted. You understand the difference between needs and wants and wealth will flow through you, rather than from you.

PRINCIPLE 4
BUILD UP YOUR MENTAL RESERVES

Protect and guard your mind by building up your mental reserves, not allowing your mind to go anywhere it wants to go. Spend time training your mind to focus and concentrate on the promises of God for your life. Speak words that will transcend your thoughts, reaching for exceedingly and abundantly above all you can ask or think. You are what you think. Therefore, think that you are the head and not the tail, you are above and not beneath, you are the lender and not the borrower. Practice mindfulness. You are what you think, and you become what you are thinking. What are you thinking? Who are you? What have you become? Now, that you are certain about who you are, begin to let your life reflect what you are thinking. The time is now to stretch the elasticity of your mind and know that True Wealth Starts in the Mind: Whatever a man sets his mind to will not be denied.

*Wealth is not about
having a lot of money;
it's about having
a lot of options.*

CHRIS ROCK

 **Angie Reed-Hogans** was born in Cleveland Ohio. She moved to Atlanta, Georgia as a child. She is the second oldest of three siblings and has one son, Michael. She previously had a career as a Delta Flight Attendant. She also excelled as a Top Producing Realtor ranked in the Top 5 percent nationwide in Atlanta with Coldwell Banker.

Angie attended Georgia State University before taking the job at Delta Airlines. She worked there nine and a half years and advanced to coordinator over flight attendant training.

Angie has hobbies of riding her motorcycle with her husband Randy Hogans and building their business. She loves developing leaders and has a team that she adores and cherishes with all her heart.

ANGIE REED-HOGANS

Mindset: Embracing The Great Shift

Growing up I remember being the kid in the bunch with the least. Chicken pot pies and free lunches were the norm for my brother and me. We grew up watching my mom work two jobs and being a product of an abusive second marriage. I had no idea that the road ahead of me would be a roller coaster ride that would prepare me for a mental shift I would one day encounter to turn my life around. My parents divorced when I was only two years old. For a period of time my brother and I ended up living with my granddad, who was handicapped from a bad car accident that killed my grandmother, aunt, and cousin. This is how we ended up moving from Ohio to Georgia. The doctors wanted him to move to a warmer climate. We were living with my granddad from the time we got to Georgia. The state felt that he wasn't capable of taking care of us and put us into the foster care system. Like clockwork, my granddad came to see us every weekend with gifts. I never knew how but my father ended up coming to Georgia to say he was going to take custody of us and handed us back over to our granddad. My father returned to Ohio the next day, once we got out of court, and we were back with our granddad. My brother and I were now happy again, reunited with granddad until our mother got to Atlanta and we moved in with her. By the time I turned 16, I started working part-time after school. I would get bored on a job quickly and go find another one that would challenge me more, pretty often. Mom always reminded me not to quit one job until I found another one, and I quickly mastered that. I guess the great shift of the mind was planted early of never being comfortable. By the time I graduated from high school, I was still undecided about what I wanted to do but I did like most say and went to college, but I really was just going through the motions. As soon as I got the job offer with the airline, I took it! I didn't return next semester to school. Facing the corporate world with no college degree, again I found myself bored with being a flight attendant. I needed a challenge, so I sought out positions to move to another department. I was told by many that I wouldn't get selected without a degree. This would be the first of many times I heard I couldn't do something. I prepared for a panel interview and climbed the corporate ladder with no college degree.

Once I had my son, I realized I didn't want to be away from him. I came to realize the corporate world just wasn't for me. I decided to think out of the box and started my second shift of mindset. I sought out to pursue a career in real estate. My family discouraged me, saying it was too saturated. For some reason, when people would tell me I couldn't do something, it gave me the fuel I needed to give it my all. This was when I started embracing the shift of the unknown to the possibilities. I quickly began observing the most successful agent at the office. She always came in early and stayed late. I noticed she was action driven. It didn't take me long to figure out I had to shift my mindset to be a player like she was. This was when I can say I really embraced a great shift in how I would think and move. I would drop my son off at school and be dressed for the day every morning. I realized you attract what you are, and I wanted to be dressed for success when I left the house. I knew to get clients, I had to talk to a lot of people. I wasn't going to be a secret agent. I had developed a work ethic so strong, my income quickly exceeded the income on my job, so I resigned from the airline. I was so afraid of change and the transition to being self-employed, but seeing other women that looked like me being successful, I just had to give it my all and see. I was determined to dive all in. I quickly became the number two agent under the example I had observed and mirrored. She had been in the business fifteen years and by my third year, I was right there with her and ranked in the top 5% for Coldwell Banker agents nationwide.

When the economy took a turn for the worse, things began to change, as did my finances. I shifted to looking for other streams of income. I landed on the platform of many MLM companies. Well, that was short-lived and didn't stick. I know I tried four to five different ones. When those didn't work, I decided to go back and interview to get my airline job back. When they said I got the job, reality kicked in for me. I've been free from a time clock and now I'm going back to one? I went home after my interview that Friday and fell on my knees to pray and ask God, "What else can I do?"

On Sunday my phone rang and it was the guy that tried to get me to do another business a whole year earlier. I knew this was a great shift of stepping out of the box and stepping into new territory. I was now changing my career and embarking upon different territory, the unknown. I would now be educating people on their finances and protecting their assets. I knew I did not have time to play around, since my mortgage was four months behind and I had spent all my savings. I was very coachable and simply ran the play I was given by my business partner that was training me. I was now in a different vehicle that would one day position me to be an example of fighting through and shifting a mindset to win in the midst of a storm. Being a type A personality and coming from being a successful realtor, I had to see results and I mean fast! I was so laser beamed on getting results that I didn't care to listen to the negative people that said what I couldn't do. I had work ethic in real estate so I knew I wasn't lazy. Where there is Passion, there is Perfection.

Once I started dating my husband, I had to make another shift of staying focused to win his support. When he realized I was all in he saw that I was going to chase my dreams with or without him. This would be the game changer for an awesome partnership ahead. Never giving excuses and keeping a big vision is how I stayed motivated. Excuses could become a distraction that could cause me to settle and get comfortable. As different storms came at me in life, I chose what to give my energy to and what not to give it to. I knew my past didn't determine my future, nor did dream killers. I surrounded myself with positive people that had the same mindset I have and that's a no-matter-what attitude. The adversity I faced on my journey prepared me to be mentally tough and embrace change, bounce back and continue the race God had put before me. Believing I can do anything I wanted to when others said I couldn't and being willing to embrace a shifting in my mind has been the beginning of awesome things yet to come.

The biggest obstacle

to wealth is fear.

People are afraid to think big,

but if you think small,

you'll only achieve

small things.

T. HARV EKER

Robert Davis was born and raised in the Bronx, NY. After he graduated from High School, he enrolled in college at South Carolina State University, where he attended four years and received a Bachelor of Arts degree in Music Education. From there he attended Radford University in Radford, Virginia, where he received a Masters of Arts degree in Piano Pedagogy.

Rob is a former teacher, basketball coach and choral director. While a teacher in Columbia, SC at W. G. Sanders middle school, he started his own Financial Services business on a part-time basis. To date, he has 20+ years' experience in financial services and is currently a National Sales Director and the owner and CEO of The Davis Group. He has served as an executive board member on the African American Leadership Council, a service organization that empowers, instructs and mentors other African Americans on how to make a six-figure income in finances. As an active member of Brookland Baptist Church, Rob has also served on the board of the Brookland Lakeview Empowerment Center.

Rob is married to his wife, Minnie and they have two children, Maya and Robbie. Rob's mission is to help North American families achieve their goals and live their dreams. His motto is: The key to being blessed is, you must first be a blessing!

ROB DAVIS

Traditional Education Isn't Enough

I was born and raised in the Patterson Houses, a large housing project in the South Bronx. I was first fed food by my parents and other family and friends as a child. Then, as we all do, I learned to feed myself. Everyone knows there is a natural importance in eating food for the body, but as I look back on my life I see I was also fed things that shaped my thoughts and beliefs on other things as well. Creating wealth was sure as hell not one of them! It was not until I was an adult well into my twenties that I realized I needed to be feeding my mind. That would ultimately determine whether or not I would live a wealthy life.

Living in the projects in the Bronx showed me poverty and how to comfortably adapt to it. Since everyone was broke, our "happy" was directly relative to our environment. I never, ever went into the city and experienced the true essence of the iconic side of New York: Manhattan, Wall Street, The Waldorf, the Ritz-Carlton or shopping on 5th Avenue. The closest I got was 42nd Street, where the $0.50 peep shows were popular, prostitution was commonplace and con artists were on the street playing Three Card Monte and perfecting the art of taking tourists' money under the guise of providing a small measure of entertainment.

My friends and I would go to see three karate movies for one price. It was usually two B-rated movies, and the main event was a classic film starring Bruce Lee. As we sat in the dank and crowded theater and watched Bruce karate-chop his way through what seemed like hundreds of bad guys, periodically we would hear someone yell out, "RAT!" Everyone would instinctively lift their feet and legs just in case the announced rat or mouse ran across your row. There were no complaints and if there were, there were no refunds; it was the way it was, and it was all we knew. It quickly became normal for our environment. Amazingly, this was one of the pastimes that we would consider a treat!

After the movies we would take the train back home to the projects, our own little slice of stability, mimicking every move we saw Bruce make onscreen on each other along the way. In our minds we were happy. We were ghetto black belts.

I remember my parents playing the numbers: the project version of today's lottery. My parents even had what was known to everyone as a dream book. The dream book was a resource that had a number that corresponded to any aspect of a person's dream. People then used whatever combination of numbers their dream prescribed to play the numbers. Ultimately, it mostly served to make the adults in my life feel like they had a more active role in their success. This was feeding me how to get rich. This was a tradition we thought would pay off financially. The flaw in that logic was that without changing or growing who you are, the probability of success is nearly impossible. My parents, family, friends and the society I experienced also taught/fed me their golden key to success. This was supposed to be the key to wealth, a great life and unlimited opportunity...but it turned out to be a great lie.

The Great Golden Lie: "Go to school/college, get a good education and get a good job." This was the mantra of my time, so much so that I did exactly that! I was the first in my family to get a Bachelor's degree or a Master's degree. Both of my degrees were in Music Education so I thought for sure I was in line to get a good job and become a teacher. After my formal education, I taught in the South Carolina public school system for seven years, maxing my salary out at a whopping $26,500 my seventh year as an educator.

Needless to say, it didn't take seven years to figure out this traditional education I was fed and ate was not healthy food. It was during my first year teaching I noticed a paycheck-to-paycheck trend developing. I had all this experience and education, I'd done what they all hadn't and told me to, yet I was going to my parents' house on weekends to wash clothes and raid the pantry. I tell people today, "I was so broke if someone tried to rob me, I'd tell them consider this practice" because I had no money!

Eventually I started doing side jobs for extra cash. I gave private piano lessons, served as a church musician, played for weddings, coached basketball and even worked in the mall at a sporting goods store one summer, all as a teacher with a Master's degree!

In the fall of 1989, during my second year of teaching, everything changed. I was invited to a table where I was being fed wealthy food for the mind! The traditional education started to become a foreign language. During my second year teaching I joined a company that was willing to pay me based on my determination and work ethic and started making money as a business owner versus an employee. This was something non-traditional, radical even... a business, not a job.

In 1989 I began my journey into entrepreneurship. It took me three years to get used to this untraditional thinking, learn the language of success and understand how I had to grow to fill this position. Roughly two years after that, in 1994, I resigned from my traditional teaching job after seven years and a meager salary of $26,500. It took me another two years to earn six figures as a business owner in 1996 and I'm blessed to have never made less than $100,000 since then. By 2008, I was making $200,000 and have never made less since! As a business, I've made over six million dollars in just 20 years. Had I stayed in my trained vocation with my coveted Master's degree and latest salary, I would have made just over $600,000. Though I didn't grow up wealthy or learning about wealth as a child or young adult or learning how to be a business owner, I began see how traditional education is simply not enough!

So what are the key areas of traditional education that aren't enough? What binds our minds? Our beliefs? Our thoughts? Our actions? What stops most people from achieving a great life? What keeps people from fighting for a life of time, freedom, and money? In this chapter I want to cover the answers!

I have learned the key to success lies in understanding there are three traditional institutions that have prohibited the average person from achieving success. Traditional institutionalism is the kryptonite to wealth!

1. Corporate America is one of the biggest traditional institutions that systematically inhibits our minds and feeds us lies about success and becoming wealthy. Society has tricked us into believing the key to success is to go to school/college, get a good education (grades) and get a good job. However, as you examine the outcome of this thinking, you won't see more wealthy people

that currently have or have ever had a job; what you tend to see is business owners! If you want to be wealthy figure out how to be a business owner and create opportunities, business partners and jobs for people so they can have a real shot at wealth. The key to being blessed is you should first be a blessing. If you help others get what they want and/or need, I truly believe God will in turn bless you with your wants and needs. The best way to benefit from the "system" is to be its creator/owner: become an owner versus working on a job. The concept of The Cash Flow Quadrant, by *Robert Kiyosaki*, is one everyone should learn as a child!

2. The banking industry is another traditional institution that misdirects our thought process about wealth while cramping our ability to create wealth. If you truly want to be wealthy versus weary, if you want to be financially independent, you must stop using the bank's savings accounts to attempt to accumulate wealth. The bank was never designed for growth of principal, but what are we fed as a child? Save where: in the bank! I remember back when there were Christmas clubs where members could save every month for 12 months and take the money out during December to buy gifts and spend money on things that depreciate. Not to mention the interest on a savings account at a bank can be as low as .0025%. No one knew enough to teach me growing up, as a young adult, through post-graduate education or even with my teaching job about Mutual Funds or any other investments. It wasn't until owning a business that I learned about proper ways to accumulate wealth and the subsequent potential and purpose of investing. I also learned about The Rule of 72 as a business owner. If you want to become wealthy you have to learn how to max out this rule and increase your knowledge of Mutual Funds.

3. Finally, the third tradition we learn as a child and adult that institutionalizes us, that keeps us from wealth is, the insurance industry and their belief on whole life insurance being a product that you should buy. This institution created a policy that stifles wealth! Whole life insurance is one of the top types of cash value policies that destroys a person's ability to build wealth. It's designed, in my opinion, to keep families in a perpetual state of starting each generation over from scratch, pretty much with no assets.

Think about it: The Federal Trade Commission in 1979 reported that "consumers of whole life policies are losing billions of dollars a year." They also state: "55 cents out of each premium dollar goes into what is essentially a savings account" (the cash value). A whole life policy builds cash value (savings) but when you die you don't receive the cash and the face amount. For example, for a face amount policy for $25,000 and a cash value of $6,000 the benefit when the insured dies is only $25,000! Not $31,000! This is how the typical whole life policy works. And that's not the only flaw in whole life insurance. Any type of insurance that builds a cash value has flaws because one affects the other in some form or fashion. Primerica teaches about the flaws and they don't offer ANY CASH VALUE POLICIES! They are the only insurance company that sells term 100% of the time. A simple way to buy insurance where there's no saving and insurance connected! I believe Primerica shouldn't be called an insurance company; Primerica should be called a blessed assurance company! Their concept: buy term and invest the difference! I have learned to build wealth by avoiding traditional policies that build cash value, and I spend less money on term with Primerica and investing in Mutual Funds versus investing in cash value policies.

As you can conclude, having your own business, investing in Mutual funds, and buying term insurance have not been the traditional way of thinking or teaching. But if you want to win and be successful, don't allow your past to dictate your future! Use your past as a book, not a sledgehammer! The process for success changes the way you think, so you can change your habits, and then the results will change. But it's hard to do better if you don't see better!

Knowledge isn't always the key when the knowledge we get is from institutions designed for people to be dependent versus independent. The challenge for you and everyone else that wants to build wealth is that you cannot continue to allow broke-focused traditions to keep you broke! Use each wealth building concept and start your journey to success now. I challenge you to get your belief level up, because you will never outperform your belief level. For me, I learned that with God all things are possible. Always remember there is both earthly wisdom and godly wisdom and those that reverence the Lord can receive both. As I continue in His will, through obedience to His commandments, I gain understanding and knowledge.

If your journey through life is to be successful now and, in the future, I believe it must begin with the acknowledgement of God and a reverence for who He is. As you obey commandments, you will be positioning yourself to gain insight to the ways of the Lord, resulting in a victorious walk.

I am a husband to my lovely wife, Minnie, for seven years and father of two lovely children, Maya and Robbie. We all have decided as a family to live a life that will one day be looked at as the start of a new tradition, one that creates wealth. I owe my wife Minnie a lot because she helped me stay focused on the next level. Because of her I understand success isn't a destination, it's a journey. She is a true help-meet and she gives me a reason to fight for a great life for our family and the next generations!!!

Keep fighting, never quit, and I will see you at the top, because the bottom is definitely too crowded.

*The person who doesn't
know where his next dollar
is coming from usually
doesn't know where his
last dollar went.*

UNKNOWN

Joyclen White Prevost is a servant leader, inspirational speaker, and empowering trainer and coach.

She's the Owner and Chief Executive Officer of Prevost Powerhouse. Joyclen is a National Sales Director with the largest marketing financial services Firm in North America.

She's dedicated to educating and transferring her knowledge, skill and confidence to business leaders and organizations teaching them to teach others how to become financially literate affecting change in communities.

Joyclen's formal education is in Business Administration and currently she's pursuing a Doctorate in Theology, to continue to teach and further advance the gospel of Jesus Christ.

She has been a successful entrepreneur for nearly 25 years. Joyclen's story has been featured in magazines, radio shows and TV. She has served as keynote speaker all over the United States reaching and inspiring thousands.

Joyclen's life is a testament of God's faithfulness as she is a survivor of two brain aneurysms.

She has authored and published two books, It's Your Life Fight For It, and Wired To Win. She is the devoted wife of Kenneth Sr., they reside in Louisiana, have two beautiful children Kenneth Jr, Keondra, and one grandchild, Kennedy.

JOYCLEN PREVOST
Don't Make Excuses

When Warren Buffett was asked how he would describe the difference between getting rich and being wealthy, his answer was short and to the point: "People seeking riches never have enough. Wealth is a state of mind."

Wealthy people always have enough. This would suggest that true wealth is an inner condition experienced long before you experience the outer manifestations of wealth. While there are those who seek reasons and logic as to why they can't, they won't, or they shouldn't, this tendency is sometimes mistaken for being realistic as they search for ways to justify why something shouldn't be without ever really trying.

However, true wealth begins with becoming... Becoming more than you have ever thought or imagined and being intentional about how you will get there. Truly wealthy people are fulfilled in possessing what really matters.

SELF AWARENESS
LIVING A PURPOSEFUL LIFE
HAVE APPRECIATION
WORK ETHIC

PERSONALLY DEVELOP

POSSESS A GENEROUS HEART AND SPIRIT

All of these characteristics are embedded in the being of a wealthy mindset.

CHARACTERISTICS OF THE TRUE WEALTHY

SELF AWARENESS

Self-awareness, simply put, having a good prospective of your personality. When you are self-aware you understand your strengths and your weaknesses. You have good judgment of others and how you are being perceived instantly. Self-awareness helps you tune into your feelings as well as the feelings and behaviors of others around you.

LIVING A PURPOSEFUL LIFE

When you are living a purposeful life, effortlessly, it just flows. You are able to tackle any obstacle and adapt to any situation set before you. You learn to move contently through life's experiences charting your own course peacefully. These individuals have core beliefs that are driven by their values and beliefs that shape their decisions. Many people's purpose can be connected to their profession or vocation, while others purpose can lie in their commitment and responsibility to their spouses, or family members.

HAVE APPRECIATION

This is vital, in my opinion, as it is one of the components human behavior craves. Along with being recognized, and being a part of something bigger than yourself, human beings want nothing more than to be appreciated. Everybody wants to be appreciated. Showing someone the feeling of gratitude and expressing admiration and approval is a human need for most people. When value is shown in one's performance and work, people are motivated to maintain and do even better. Just as their personal satisfaction increases, productivity increases. Appreciation is truly a difference maker and a key component to building relationships. In relationships where someone does not feel appreciated you will soon experience problems. Showing appreciation whether it's in the work place or to a love one, it just makes people feel good about their contribution.

WORK ETHIC

Here are some characteristics of good work ethic: consistency, punctuality, teamwork, cooperation, attendance, high productivity, professionalism, superior quality work, and a strong determination to succeed.

Strong work ethic is a character trait. The best way to learn something is by doing. You're going to get your hands dirty. This is a necessity to succeed. It won't be good enough to just start. You must be a finisher, and to be a finisher, you must have a strong work ethic. Talent, Intellect, and Charisma will all have roles along your success journey, but all must be accompanied by an insane work ethic.

Disciplined work ethic is a set of values centered on the importance of work and manifested by determination to work hard.

This is a skill that can be developed and taught with good habits and proper motivation.

"There's no substitution for hard work". Thomas Edison

PERSONALLY DEVELOP

Personal development is an ongoing process. It's a concentrated interest on yourself to grow and mature.

This will require stepping up spiritually emotionally, physically and financially.

Some ways to personally develop would be to have clear written down goals for yourself that are time stamped.

Personally developing you will require some investment both monetarily, and in effort.

You can purchase books, listen to CD's, podcast, sound cloud, watch videos, and read autobiographies of people who have excelled. Working from an appointment book, getting an accountability partner, as well as enlisting mentorship are all sure ways of growing and developing yourself personally.

Taking these action steps will help you with organization, time management, and development of new skill sets needed to propel you to next levels along your success journey. Just keep going and you will keep learning and growing.

POSSESS A GENEROUS HEART AND SPIRIT

Generosity of the heart is demonstrated in somebody who is free and happy to show kindness. They are willing to give food, money or time. Somebody that's unselfish and willing to go above and beyond what is expected. Generosity of the heart is giving of oneself and an act of kindness, love and compassion.

Somebody with a generous spirit will embrace differences with an acceptance of others. They genuinely are happy for others good fortune regardless of their own. They are devoid of jealousy, envy or strife and they don't think ill of others and rarely will you ever hear disparaging remarks about others. This is someone who is nonjudgmental, tolerating different beliefs, ideas and behaviors.

Someone with a generous spirit will tend to be positive of others versus looking for what's wrong or negative.

They tend to look for and assume the best in people and treat all people with the same degree of respect and acceptance.

STOP PROCRASTINATING

Procrastinators commonly make excuses for delaying and putting things off. They tend to think they always have more time than they actually do. Some of the thing's procrastinators say to afford themselves the opportunity to put off is, I work well under pressure, I will take care of that tomorrow, I don't know where to begin.

Distractions are huge reasons why procrastinators wait until a later time. Those distractions come in various forms like emails, text messages, social media, conference calls, Skyping people, and side tasks.

Some studies have shown that because of smart phones, internet, and, even gossip, many employees typically work less than five hours in a full work day.

Procrastinators often times are found immersed in unimportant activities while things they should be doing are put off or never get done.

Some reasons individuals find it easier to put off and even stop prematurely are;

> Fear
> Not Focused
> Uncertainty
> Not energetic
> Perfectionism

Don't know how to do all the steps, so they do none

People typically put things off because they don't want to do them or they have to do them. Procrastination leads to problems when postponing things that should be taken care of now.

True wealthy mindsets realize they don't have a day to wait, not an hour or even one minute to wait.

Procrastination is an illness and must be dealt with to get the most out of your life.

Some things you can do to begin your process of healing:

- Recognize when you put off you are a procrastinator
- Have a sense of urgency
- Daily have a Things-to-do list
- Delegate things others can take care of for you

Ninety-nine percent of failures come from people who have the habit of making excuses and putting things off.

I am reminded of a specific prayer I prayed some time ago for a better life in which I would have additional freedom and control of my schedule with more income and a life of options that I could only dream about. During this time, I was a medical transcriptionist working in a hospital for a total of ten years. When my business opportunity was presented, I really thought my husband was better suited because I was quiet and very inward. I initially wanted to make an excuse for why I could not do what I needed to do to obtain a better quality of life that would give us more choices and the time with each other I desired.

Having a wealthy mindset requires you to say, before you ever start, it won't get too tough for me, quitting is not an option, and excuses don't count.

My husband Kenneth and I partnered in life 34 years ago and 23 of those years we've been partnered in business. We have two wonderful children Kenneth and Keondra, both are successful young adults, one precious angel, our granddaughter Kennedy Gabrielle

They truly are the great investment and reasons why we do it all.

It has now been 23 years, but I remember it like it was yesterday. There I was, faced with an opportunity of a life time that promised to change our lives forever, and I immediately started to question whether I could do something different, make all the necessary changes, or even be the right type of person. I thought about making an excuse.

Instead, I realized God had answered my prayer, and it was time for me to accept the gift that would require many changes and would ultimately change our life for generations to come. The hardest thing about new endeavors is always getting started, but right now is always the best time to get started going in the right direction.

I had to make personal development a priority for myself and imagine the inevitable—change—had to happen. If I was willing to grow past my limitations and do the necessary work, I could build a successful business and ultimately develop a wealthy mindset. I have spent several decades and a percentage of my income investing in a library of books, seminars, workshops, and leadership conferences. There have been years of turning my car into a classroom as I listened to tapes, CDs of winning examples and autobiographies of leaders and winners who had done exemplary things with their lives.

EXCUSES WON'T MATTER

Several years after we started our family business, a major storm, Hurricane Katrina, destroyed my city. There were no emails and ATMs; businesses were destroyed and there were many losses of life. It was a city under siege. Our city suffered a category five hurricane and then a flood. We had to relocate and leave our city for several years. There I was in Houston, Texas, a major metropolis and new surrounding for me, my family, and many of my teammates.

It was as if overnight life had changed drastically, and my life as I knew it would never be the same. We were forced to transition and make decisions like finding a new school for my daughter, looking for a new office for my business, and even finding a new home in another state. We were faced with establishing our new way of life in unfamiliar territory. Nothing was the same, and to say I was very uncomfortable would be an understatement. I could have easily made excuses, as some days it seemed as though I was running on empty.

It was during these years that my faith in God and Bishop I.V. Hillard's teachings where we fellowshipped while in Texas would be like fresh air and would pull me up again because I knew excuses didn't count, no matter how hard it got. It would also be during this time, I learned like no other: "What really matters never changes." This would be the very moment I would need to remind myself of why I went in business for myself and started something new. We still had our faith in God, our health and strength, a great business opportunity that we could take anywhere we went, and most of all, a wealthy mindset. There was no time to give up; it was time to get help. I had a choice to make, and that choice entailed reinventing myself or making an excuse as to why I could not reinvent myself.

EXCUSE: Webster defines excuse as

1. an attempt to lessen the blame attaching to (a fault or offense); seek to defend or justify. Synonyms: justify, defend, make excuses for, make a case for, explain, rationalize, condone, vindicate, warrant.
2. release (someone) from a duty or requirement, exempt.

Although the definitions for the word excuse are extensive, none of them seemed valid enough for me to throw in the towel and quit on my goals, dreams, and my family. I chose to reinvent myself without making excuses. Assessing my situation, I realized excuses don't help you in any way, and after a while people just get tired of hearing them. It's been stated that excuses are a lazy person's best friend, and it's a friend that will never help you get where you need or want to go in life.

The following are some of the most common excuses I've heard:

I don't know what I want
I'm afraid
I haven't done that before
It's too hard
I really don't have time
It won't work for me
I'm broke
It's not my fault
I don't have a car
Nobody believes in me
I can't get a break
I'm too old
I'm not educated
I live in the wrong area
I'll do it later
I don't know how
I don't know anybody
I never had anything
I can't do it on my own
Nobody cares about me
No one will help me
I don't have the right relationships

I'll never make it
I keep making the same mistakes
I'm too young
I don't have friends
I'll never find the right person
I don't look the part
Nobody likes me
I don't have any support
I'm too shy and introverted
I can't keep up with technology
I'll never make it
I'll never break this habit
It's too late for me

EXCUSES, EXCUSES, EXCUSES

Your reasons have to become bigger than any excuse you can make.

TAKING TOTAL RESPONSIBILITY

It has been said that "excuses are crutches for the uncommitted." I wholeheartedly agree, as I realize excuses are usually reasons for trying to get someone to cut us some slack. I have a strong stance on excuses. Consequently, I don't give excuses. I don't even want to hear them because your explanation will really cause the excuse to make sense to me, so don't even tell me. I already know that excuses won't count, and you can't deposit them! Only what you get done will matter.

In some instances, it's sometimes as simple as saying, "I'm sorry," rather than added dialog, finger pointing or playing the blame game.

True wealth really does begin in the mind. The scripture teaches us that God has already given us the power to get wealth. That means we already possess it. It lives on the inside of us, and the speed with which it will manifest itself on the outside lies within our ability to make no excuses.

EXCUSES DON'T COUNT

Within God's Word, there is the 'Parable of the Talents,' in which the master called his three servants and entrusted them with his property. They were each admonished to go and reproduce. There were two servants who were faithful and did what was expected of them, but the third servant did not. When the master returned, the unproductive servant made an excuse as to why he did not reproduce or achieve a return on the master's investment. He said, "I knew you were a hard man." He made an excuse, and he was rebuked. Moreover, what he had was taken from him and given to the more profitable servant. Because he was more disciplined and focused on the task at hand, the profitable servant undoubtedly stepped out of his comfort zone to achieve extraordinary results. He was awarded with true wealth and abundance, but the unprofitable servant was rewarded with lack.

> [28]"So take the bag of gold from him and give it to the one who has ten bags. [29]For whoever has will be given more, and they will have an abundance, whoever does not have, even what they have will be taken from them.[30]And throw the worthless servant outside, into the darkness, where there will be weeping and gnashing of teeth."
> New International Version, Matthew 25: 28-30

From this story, one can readily see that, "your comfort zone will equal your wealth zone." You have to be uncomfortable to do anything extraordinary.

"Ninety-nine percent of failures come from people who have the habit of making excuses."

WHEN ALL EXCUSES ARE ELIMINATED:

- CHANGES WILL BE EMINENT
- COMMITMENT TO YOUR OWN HAPPINESS
- COMFORT ZONES WILL BE SHATTERED
- CHARACTER WILL BE CHALLENGED
- CONSISTENT WORK WILL BE NECESSARY
- CONSTANT ASSAULT ON EXCUSES

During a very challenging time, we had to reset, cut our losses and keep on going. With very little insight into the difficulty of the huge task before us, we went to work like never before. I became extremely focused on what I wanted. The life I dreamed about was not cancelled with that storm. With several leaders dispersed across the country, I realized that my opportunity was now even bigger, because my business had been expanded, forced to, but none the less still expanded. Our organization was now spread over a number of cities and six states.

In November 2008, thirty-six months later we experienced tremendous growth, breaking barriers and making history, promoting three additional vice presidents. We solidified our organization, The Prevost Powerhouse, as a National expansion team, and my husband and I were promoted to National Sales Directors, Office of Supervisory Jurisdiction and earned full ownership status of our franchise.

True wealth starts the minute you set your mind on success. You must be motivated and have stamina to succeed.

Practice daily affirmations, get an accountability partner, mentorship, and take the necessary action. No action, equals no results. Embrace the bad with the good.

Problems and opposition are common to life, but you must be willing to face your fears and put aside any excuse and go after what you want. Your mind is engineered to find solutions to problems and difficult things as long as you don't let yourself off the hook and make excuses. Success is reserved for those who wake up everyday and persevere, and true wealth is when you wake up and realize you are totally responsible for your own wealthy mindset and life, and the power resides on the inside of you.

Having a wealthy mindset is prosperous. Prosperity is nothing missing nothing lacking.

True wealth starts in the mind and when you have it you can win again and again.

Winners are not afraid

of losing. But losers are.

Failure is part of the

process of success.

People who avoid failure

also avoid success.

ROBERT KIYOSAKI

Bill Orender was born and raised in Chicago. He graduated from Eastern Illinois University with a Bachelor of Science in Business and an MBA from Northern Illinois University.

He is married to Carol Orender and has 4 children.

He began work in financial services in 1974 in Atlanta with A. L. Williams. Bill attained the Certified Financial Planner designation in 1977.

Bill and Carol moved to Dallas, Texas in 1978 to open the first out of state office for A. L. Williams.

Bill is a Senior National Sales Director and has over 150 Regional Vice Presidents in Primerica in 30 states.

BILL ORENDER

A Desire To Be Somebody...
Where It All Starts

As the title of this book suggests, true wealth STARTS IN THE MIND.

Whatever man puts his mind to will not be denied. When man puts his mind on BEING SOMEBODY their world changes and they are never the same. The phrase "I WANT TO BE SOMEBODY SO BAD IT BORDERS ON BEING AN OBSESSION" changed my world.

While in my early twenties I never thought much about my life and what I wanted to be. If I did any thinking at all it was about what I wanted to have or get, never about what I wanted to BE. When I heard the phrase "BE SOMEBODY," something in my soul moved. In my entire life I'd never heard the topic of, Being Somebody, mentioned. Once I did, it was like the old saying, "When the student is ready, the teacher appears."

WHAT IS IT LIKE TO WANT TO BE SOMEBODY?

I am convinced the desire to be Somebody is a primal longing waiting to be unleashed within everyone. Wanting to be Somebody is etched in our souls and we can never run away from that. Not to pursue being Somebody can haunt people all their lives. We are hardwired to be Somebody and no matter how we try to sublimate it, it keeps resurfacing.

A Somebody wants to be INVOLVED IN SOMETHING BIGGER than just themselves. There is a yearning to make a difference with their lives.

Wanting to be Somebody makes you want to BE THE BEST YOU CAN BE and stimulates the personal growth necessary to fit your dreams. A Somebody believes that becoming better makes the world better.

When was the last time, if ever, YOU CRIED because you wanted to be Somebody? A Somebody has TEARS in their eyes because being a Somebody is something they want to be so badly.

We must understand that we are all CREATED TO HAVE MEANING in our lives. A Somebody is ADMIRED AND RESPECTED, yearns and works to accomplish that ideal.

A Somebody doesn't want to disappoint people. Abraham Lincoln said, "I am where I am today because people believed in me and I didn't want to let them down." Can you stand to live your life not working toward being a Somebody?

Who is it YOU don't want to let down? Who believes in you so much that you work hard to maintain their respect? Your spouse? Your children? Your parents? A dear friend?

CORNERSTONE PHRASES THAT INSPIRE A PERSON TO BECOME A SOMEBODY:

- I want to be Somebody so bad it borders on being an obsession.
- I want to make my life COUNT.
- I want to make a DIFFERENCE with my life.
- I want to live a REMARKABLE life.
- I want to live a life of SIGNIFICANCE.
- I want my life to be MEANINGFUL.
- I want to leave this world a BETTER PLACE.
- I want to MAKE A NAME for myself.
- I want to DO SOMETHING that means something.
- I want to STAND OUT in this world.
- I want my tombstone to say "STUD."
- I want to be RESPECTED by people I respect.
- I want to be ADMIRED by those important to me.
- I want to be a person of HONOR, DIGNITY and RESPECT.
- I want a to live a life of MEANING and PURPOSE.

A SOMEBODY OR A NOBODY?

The opposite of a Somebody is a "nobody."

The opposite of living a life that counts is living life being a no – 'count.

The opposite of living a life on purpose is living a life by accident.

The opposite of making a difference is living an indifferent life.

The opposite of living a life of meaning is living a life without intention.

The opposite of a life of significance is a life of insignificance.

"I WANT TO BE SOMEBODY SO BAD."

Art Williams is the founder of the worlds' largest financial services marketing company. He has mentored countless legendary leaders in his company and his quotes are the foundation for many changed lives. His company was built on one monumental quote: "I WANT TO BE SOMEBODY SO BAD THAT IT BORDERS ON BEING AN OBSESSION." A desire to be somebody can't be explained. It can only be experienced. This obsession leads to a relentless pursuit that won't abate.

A Somebody would say, "Believe in your heart that you're meant to live a life full of passion, purpose, magic and miracles." (Roy T. Bennett)

A Somebody has an enormous CRAVING to succeed. They don't just WANT to be Somebody, THEY HAVE TO! They would be miserable if they didn't strive for it. They do it because they INSIST on it.

HOW DO YOU BECOME A SOMEBODY?

A Somebody makes other people's lives better, someone who makes a difference. They leave this world a BETTER PLACE because they were here.

We are told to be servants. Luke 22:26 (NIV) explains it perfectly. "...the greatest among you should be like the youngest, and the one who rules like the one who serves."

Interestingly, many people talk about serving, but what does that mean? As Rabbi Daniel Lapin states, "When you make someone's life better you are serving them." In fact, the Rabbi says that God created business to force us to serve one another. He explains that making money in business is a measure of whether or not you are SERVING. "Why does it surprise us when a good and loving God rewards us financially for serving His people? God created business to make sure we are good to one another."

A SOMEBODY PREPARES EVERY DAY.

All success comes when a person PREPARES in advance to succeed.

A Somebody moves forward with a mindset that fixes in their mind a detailed plan of action to accomplish their objectives and goals.

A Somebody then works their plan twelve to sixteen hours a day until they achieve their dreams. And when they are not working at it, they are THINKING ABOUT IT.

Somebodies are PREDISPOSED to succeed. They put on their track shoes and shorts, ready to run their race. Being prepared at all times for anything and everything is essential.

A SOMEBODY WANTS A LIFE OF SIGNIFICANCE.

The greatest fear in life is death. In one list I came across, the second greatest fear is living a life of insignificance. A Somebody wakes up every day and fights to be the person they should be. Or, as I've heard Art Williams say, "Call me anything but average and ordinary."

That's the kind of determination a Somebody has to have. In the end, living a LIFE OF SIGNIFICANCE carries with it eternal rewards, measured by the lives around them that they've made better. Another benefit in bettering lives is that they also better their own lives.

HOW WILL YOU BE REMEMBERED?

Many people walk in and out of your life. A Somebody leaves footprints on your heart. We all have friends and loved ones, but certain special ones we can never forget. Of all the people that have passed through our life, how many can we say actually made a difference in our world because they were here? How many can we say were essential to how our lives turned out?

A Somebody measures their life by the number of people that measure themselves against them.

A SOMEBODY SEES THEMSELVES INVOLVED IN SOME-THING BIGGER THAN THEMSELVES.

Perhaps you're familiar with the aphorism, "He who has a WHY to live can bear almost any HOW."

A Somebody doesn't see business only as a thing they are doing or a job they are performing. They see a CRUSADE, a need, a calling, an assignment that puts a fire in their belly. As Art Williams would say, "I don't know why, but my butt is always burning." They are "cause" and "crusade" driven. They see people hurting and are driven to do something about it.

Art Williams stated, "Having a crusade and righting wrongs gives you the extra courage to do the unthinkable." It's what Dennis Kimbro calls that special kind of "courage that enables you to overcome all trials and disappointments and have a single unwavering aim." A Somebody's crusade starts with COMMITMENT. They find their genius when they are fully committed to a cause. They know it would be selfish to coast.

A SOMEBODY SENSES THAT SPECIAL MOMENT THAT IS UNIQUE TO THEM.

Winston Churchill brilliantly said, "There comes a special moment in everyone's life, a moment for which that person was born. That special opportunity, when he seizes it, will fulfill his mission, a mission for which he is uniquely qualified. In that moment he finds GREATNESS. It is his finest hour."

A Somebody thinks, "If not me, who? If not now, when?" There is a timer in the head of a Somebody that is counting down how many good years they have left. They are competing against the clock of their life, like an hourglass where the sand is visibly demonstrating how time is slipping by. A Somebody is NOT CASUAL with their purpose or their time on this earth and thus they never become a casualty or a drifter.

WANTING TO BE SOMEBODY MAKES YOU EVALUATE WHERE YOU STAND IN THE STATUS QUO.

As Steve Jobs said when he spoke at Stanford University's graduation commencement, "For the past 33 years I have looked in the mirror every morning and asked myself: 'If today were the last day of my life would I want to do what I am about to do today?' And whenever the answer has been 'No' for too many days in a row, I know I need to change something."

The life we create and feed is the living reflection of what's inside us. A Somebody cares how their life's harvest will turn out. An abundant harvest means you've lived an abundant life.

A SOMEBODY LIVES A MONUMENT LIFE AND BECOMES A MT. RUSHMORE FIGURE FOR OTHERS TO FOLLOW.

A world-famous journalist, Edward H. Murrow, is an example of a Mt. Rushmore Somebody. When he died, his colleague and friend Eric Sevareid said of him, "He was a shooting star, and we will live in his afterglow a very long time."

That's the effect a Somebody has on those around him. As the old saying goes, "When the tide rises it lifts all the boats with it." When you decide to be a Somebody all sorts of people become buoyed by that decision, and they now have a hero that elevates all who need up-lifting.

As has been said, "He is the kind of person that comes along once in a lifetime. Fortunately, he came along in our lifetime."

Or, "We all have friends and loved ones. He is the one we can never forget."

Or, "How many can say they made a difference or say this world is a better place because they were here?"

Or, "He was totally essential to how my life turned out."

That's why a Somebody is enthroned on the personal Mt. Rushmore of so many lives.

SERIOUS QUESTIONS THAT GUIDE US TO LIVE A SOMEBODY LIFE:

- Why should you become obsessed with making others' lives better?
- Why should you make a difference with your life?
- Why should you leave this world a better place?
- Why is it important that you become Somebody?
- Is your desire to become Somebody on the verge of being an obsession?

A SOMEBODY IS ALWAYS REMEMBERED.

People remember where they were when…

John F. Kennedy was assassinated.

John Lennon, Michael Jackson and Princess Diana died.

Martin Luther King, Jr. was assassinated.

A Somebody lives their lives for others and can never be forgotten. Your purpose must be FOUGHT for. A purpose and a mission are not for the faint of heart. Working your purpose isn't cheap, fast and easy. It requires RESILIENCE, GRIT, RESOLVE and COMMITMENT to your purpose for as long as it takes to get the job done.

As Carlyle said, "A man without a purpose is like a ship without a rudder; a waif; a nothing; a no man. Have a purpose in life, and, having it, throw such strength of mind and muscle into your work as God has given you."

Think of Noah. He made a 120-year long-term COMMITMENT to his project. His purpose was fused with his commitment. Genesis 6:22 (NIV) states that "Noah did everything just as God commanded him." FOR 120 YEARS!

Many times, our purpose demands us to be used to an even greater capacity than our desire to be used. A worthy purpose at times is a burden and not a blessing. The blessing may come years after many burdens are dealt with. Like many authors say, "I don't like to write, I love to have written." Or, as legendary football coach Tom Landry said, "I do 90% of the things I don't like to do to get the other 10% that I love so much." As their coach he also pushed men toward their own purpose. The job of a football coach is to make men do what they don't want to do in order to achieve what they've always wanted to be.

Being Somebody is your PURPOSE, it is your CALLING, it is your GIFT. It causes you to make other people's lives better. A Somebody doesn't have to impress others with their purpose because God didn't put the purpose into another person's heart, only the heart of that particular person. Your purpose is SUPREME and UNIQUE to you.

Just as the body needs food, water and oxygen, our mind and soul need a mission, a purpose, a goal. The Danish philosopher Soren Kierkegaard wrote, "Nothing can make a person sick sooner than feeling useless, unwanted, unchallenged and unneeded." Just as without a vision the people perish, without a purpose we will never be a Somebody.

A SOMEBODY ALWAYS ASKS, WHAT MATTERS?

Somebodies don't major in minor things. Don't get caught up in all the clutter that slows down everybody else. Keep asking yourself, "Is what I'm doing today going to lead me where I want to be tomorrow?"

A Somebody sees adversity as a speed bump, while a nobody sees it as a brick wall. Harvard professor Randy Pausch said, "The brick walls are there for a reason. The brick walls are not there to keep us out. The brick walls are there to give us a chance to show how badly we want something. Because the brick walls are there to stop the people who don't want it badly enough. They're there to stop other people."

Having a MAGNIFICENT OBSESSION can wonderfully serve you. A purpose is a gift that propels you, that inspires you, that creates its own strength necessary to give you the MOTIVATION to accomplish the objectives that the purpose demands. It makes you all you can be because without it the greatness inside you lies dormant, awaiting that special something. A desire to be Somebody carries within itself all the ingredients necessary to accomplish great things.

BEING A SOMEBODY THAT YOU ARE PROUD OF AND OF WHOM YOUR FAMILY IS PROUD IS EVERYTHING.

When was the last time you heard a parent, or anyone you respect, say they were PROUD of you? Have you ever been desperate for someone, anyone, to recognize you in a special way and say, "I'm proud of you?"

During the recognition sections of meetings, I've attended I've seen grown men with tears in their eyes come on stage to get a $25 trophy. They have souls that have never felt special. They have ears that have never heard glowing comments about their performance.

Down deep we all yearn for recognition and are willing to work for that recognition. When someone tells you, they are proud of you, that is the beginning of becoming a Somebody.

A SOMEBODY WAS ONCE A NOBODY.

"If you consider yourself a nobody and do nothing to improve yourself to become a somebody, you truly will end up being a nobody. You must understand the power and capacity of every soul for self-improvement." (John Vandenberg)

A Somebody has a burning desire to IMPROVE themselves. A Somebody reads books because they know they are one book better than before they read it. Can you get 10 books better every year? Over a lifetime you can be hundreds of books better. Leaders are readers. If you tie your arm to your body and leave it there long enough it will atrophy, and you will permanently lose the use of that arm. As the adage says, "Use it or lose it."

A nobody can turn into a Somebody by reading about, listening to, and studying the Somebodies they admire and want to emulate. Abraham Lincoln said, "I shall study and prepare myself so that when my chance comes, I will be ready." Everyone has a cause that matters to them. "They made a difference in my life" is one of the greatest compliments any of us can receive.

A SOMEBODY HAS A DEEP SENSE OF DOING SOMETHING SPECIAL WITH THEIR LIVES.

All Somebodies have a deep sense of having only one life to live and wanting to live the best life possible. They have a deep DESIRE to leave this world a better place by creating the best version of themselves. They also have a deep-seated fear of waking up at an older age and saying, "Is this all there is?"

A Somebody almost tends to take life too seriously and wonders why other people don't feel the same. They often feel as if they're going down a one-way street the wrong way because they don't understand other people and other people don't understand them. As Collis Temple states, "To be great, you had better have a VENDETTA with mediocrity."

Art Williams said, "Call me anything but average and ordinary." When you want to be Somebody an ordinary existence is like a slow death. Mediocrity is like quicksand that slowly consumes and sucks the life out of you. It's impossible to explain because the desire to be Somebody comes from deep down in a place that is indescribable. It's when your SOUL and your DESTINY come together and provide a spiritual dimension to all you do.

VOCABULARY OF A SOMEBODY.

A Somebody has a special and unique vocabulary. They use uncommon words to have an uncommon life. Their words define the character it takes to live a Somebody life.

Words that define a Somebody are:

> Grit Fortitude Stud Overcome
> Tenacity Courage Prevail Irrepressible
> Will Vigor Resilience Determination
> Passion Drive Mettle Stamina
> Destiny Resolve Invincible Voracious
> Intrepid Crusader

ART WILLIAMS ON BEING SOMEBODY:

"Being Somebody and doing something with your life and something that you are proud of and having a reason to get up in the morning is just EVERYTHING."

Art, in the book *Locker Room Notes*, said:

- "I want to make a difference in peoples' lives."
- "I wasn't supposed to just exist."

- "I wasn't put on this earth to be a half-butt."
- "I want to be a part of something great."
- "I want to be good for something instead of good for nothing."
- "Everybody wants to be Somebody."
- "I want to be Somebody. I was put on this earth to be a Somebody. I'm paranoid about being Somebody."
- "I grew up believing that down deep everyone wants to be Somebody. Everyone wants to look back on his life and say, 'I mattered at something.' To look back on your life and say, 'I was proud of who I was. My life on this earth was worthwhile, I did something most people were not willing to do. I'm proud of me. I'm proud I stood for something. I'm proud of what I've done.'"
- "It's not having a lot of money, or houses, cars and yachts, or giving away a lot of money." That is just a very small part of it.
- "I think being a Somebody is looking in the mirror and saying, 'I fought a good fight; I did something I didn't think that I could do.'"
- "It's when your spouse looks at you and says, 'I'm glad I got you.' Your kids look at you and say, 'I'm proud of my mom and dad; they're special.'"
- "To be Somebody you can't wimp out or throw in the towel."
- "To be Somebody you have to lay it on the line one last time."

FINAL THOUGHTS.

When a person wants to be Somebody so bad it borders on being an obsession they stand out from the masses.

As Thoreau said, "The mass of men lead lives of quiet desperation." For a person who wants to be Somebody, the desperation can't be quiet any longer.

The object for which we strive tells the story of our life, and the life of a Somebody tells their own story. Your life will either be a great example or a terrible warning.

A Somebody wants their life to be a great example. A Somebody knows their life and their door of opportunity is fleeting. They feel an URGENCY and have a "do it now" mindset. "I charge you; once you have the dream, decide to begin and begin right away. Wait for nobody to blow whistles for you to start." (Israelmore Ayivor)

A Somebody wants to change the world and people who are crazy enough to think they can change the world are the only ones who do.

Wealth is the ability

to fully experience life.

HENRY DAVID THOREAU

Sedrick T. Thomas is an entrepreneur, inspirational speaker and author. He began his career at the age of 23. He has 35 years of experience in the Financial Industry. Since that time, he has assisted thousands of families to become properly protected, debt free and financially independent. Today Sedrick has earned the esteemed position of National Sales Director with his company. Sedrick has 25 Regional Offices throughout the United States and in 2017 he was honored to be inducted on the prestigious "Wall of Fame".

Sedrick is in high demand as a trainer and mentor with speaking engagements throughout the United States. He had penned his first self-development book "The God System: God's Keys to Manifestation."

A lifelong New Orleans native, Sedrick is a graduate of the prestigious McDonough 35 High School and the University of New Orleans. He credits his time at these institutions as pivotal stepping stones that led to his present success.

Sedrick counts most precious to him, Tanya, his wife of 30 years and his 5 children. They are the driving force behind all of his accomplishments.

Sedrick T. Thomas

The Creative Power
of Our Thoughts

"What we think we say, what we say we believe, what we believe we see, what we see we create; therefore, always think about what you are thinking about." ~ Sedrick T. Thomas

God said let there be light, and there was light. Genesis 1:3

WHAT WE THINK WE SAY

There are three things that create our reality:

1. Thoughts we have
2. Words we speak
3. Actions that we take

Our thoughts have creative power. Everything starts with a thought. After the thought, words are spoken. Once you speak something, you set the wheels in motion for the action to follow. This is the process of creating and ultimately, if you believe the words that are spoken and follow with action, you will have what you are seeking. Some call this manifestation, but I refer to it as the creative power of thought.

IT STARTED WITH ONE THOUGHT

Have you ever thought of business ownership? Thought what it would be like to be Bill Gates, the owner of Microsoft; Shawn Carter (aka JayZ), the owner of RocNation; or Oprah Winfrey, the owner of HARPO? Each one of them now enjoys a life of freedom, time and money, but all of their journeys began with the creative power of a thought.

When I was in high school, I came up with the idea of starting a group with some of my buddies. This group would not be a singing group, a rap group, or a dance group. We would not be like the status quo. This group would be like no other group that existed at my school. We would be a business club. At age the age of 16, I was already thinking about becoming a successful businessman. Because I spoke about it to others and then put the action behind my words, we started a business club.

It was a successful business club, but part of the success of the club was attributed to my parents. I had seen business people, business ownership and entrepreneurship all of my life. When I was a young boy, I began dreaming of becoming a successful businessman, wearing fine suits, sitting in board rooms, and conversing with colleagues, making big decisions. This was attractive and ignited intense desire in me, but it all began with the thought of me one day becoming a successful businessman.

I saw my parents in business ownership roles. My mother, Delores Thomas, was the owner of a daycare center and my father, John Henry Thomas, was a gospel preacher and he pastored several churches in New Orleans. Throughout my childhood and all of my school years I saw my parents control their own time and destiny. They were their own bosses. They never had to ask anyone to take off or to go on vacations. They were in control of their own schedules. My siblings and I had the benefit of having our mother and father present and very involved in all of our activities. This flexibility was a luxury that afforded the opportunity to have very active roles in our daily routines, like transporting us to and from school and being classroom mentors and community role models. Because my parents were business owners, my family benefited from many liberties monetarily that most of my friends and some family members did not. As a young man, I was often told things like, "you're going to be somebody special, young man; you're going places in your life." I believed that it would happen for me.

Belief is a key component to the creative power of thought. One can have an idea and can even speak aloud about that idea, but in order to begin to invoke action, one must believe that they can achieve that idea. God confirms the power of belief in Matthew 17:20—He replied, "Because you have so little faith. Truly I tell you, if you have faith as small as a mustard seed, you can say to this mountain, move from here to there and it will move. Nothing will be impossible for you." God said NOTHING would be impossible for us to achieve with belief, therefore every thought is an attainable thing. But you can think a thought, believe it, speak it and put action behind it and still be out of alignment with what you really want to happen in your life.

During my sophomore year in college I started working for an engineering firm as an intern. Upon my completion of the internship the firm hired me permanently and I spent six years there. What I loved most was the freedom to be creative with design, and the opportunities were limitless in terms of the ideas that could be birthed and flourish. With bittersweet feelings I found myself dying on the inside with the confinement, controlled environment, and limited interaction with people. It did not take very long for me to realize this profession was nothing like the dreams I had envisioned for my future. The seed to become a successful businessman had been planted when I was a young boy and I was living in direct opposition to that thought. The structure, the routine, and the mundane, humdrum, existence of each day seemed like an eternity to me.

During my tenure at the firm I observed the people I worked for. They were third generation business owners and they were all free. Frequently they would travel on lavish vacations all over the world. They would travel in clusters with lots of family members all at one time. This is what I wanted for my life.

Here I was 23 years of age, working at a prominent firm and very disenchanted. Having a wealthy mindset starts with having the right kind of mindset. When your heart is right and you have done all you can do, God is required to help you. I stayed positive and kept going to work daily and was often complimented as one of the most diligent young professionals at the firm. It was during this time I heard an advertisement on the radio that there was a seminar being held at the Doubletree Hotel in the City of New Orleans. The seminar was teaching people how to write business plans. Eager to learn all I could about business, I attended the seminar.

While there I met some dynamic individuals, Francis Warren and Naomi White. They were Regional Vice Presidents and invited me to an opportunity meeting. I attended the meeting two days later. Little did I know this would be the meeting that would change my life forever. The leaders there spoke the language I had been confessing. I loved the environment and the people were all very personable and professional. It did not seem as though it could get any better, and then I heard them say I could own my own business. I joined their team that night.

I realized that this experience, along with my upbringing, had stimulated the wheel of entrepreneurship. The thought of becoming a successful businessman made me happy. I got excited about working very hard and becoming a business owner. The best part was I could control it with my thoughts. With every thought we think, we are designing our future.

Today I'm a successful businessman who owns my own firm and I am blessed with the opportunity to mentor and groom others with the same opportunity. It all started with the thought that it could happen, and I held onto that hope until an opportunity was presented. I was not willing to settle for anything less. Everything starts with a thought. The happiness I know today started with the quality of my thoughts.

WHAT WE SAY WE BELIEVE

Today some of my practices are, if I have a negative thought, or thoughts that don't serve me well, I can recognize them immediately and replace them. I've taught my family and countless others how to do the same.

My baby girl Jade was a freshman in high school and she was making C's and D's and perfectly okay with it. When I had enough of it, I confronted her and asked her, "Baby, why are you performing poorly?" She said to me, "Daddy, just accept it, I'm a C and D student." I immediately asked her who told her that, and I further told her I thought she was an A and B student. I wanted to encourage her to start speaking a different language and to believe for better. To let my daughter know how much I believed in her I told her I would give her $100 for every A she got. She smiled and with a different bounce charted a new course. Jade began getting A's and B's and graduated high school with a high B average. She continued her education at Louisiana State University and graduated with a Bachelor's degree in Marketing. Jade broke the barrier of her limiting beliefs. She started believing she could, so she did.

The opposite of this empowering practice is the practice of limiting beliefs. Limiting beliefs are those thoughts which constrain us in some way. Just by entertaining those thoughts we believe them, and subsequently we do the things that inhibit us. We impoverish our lives by doing so. Unfortunately, this is done more often than not. The great thing is that we have the power to stop those limiting thoughts by simply changing our language. For example:

If one says: I'M AFRAID TO LOVE AGAIN BECAUSE I MIGHT GET HURT...

REPLACE it with: I will love like I've never been hurt before because when I open up my heart it attracts the right kind of love in my life.

If one says: I DON'T WANT TO ASK FOR WHAT I WANT, BECAUSE THEY MAY SAY NO...

REPLACE it with: Every NO gets me closer to the YES. No just means not today.

If one says: I CAN'T TRUST PEOPLE BECAUSE I'VE BEEN LIED TO...

REPLACE it with: I can never have a meaningful relationship if I don't trust.

If one says: I'M AFRAID TO TRY BECAUSE I MIGHT FAIL...

REPLACE it with: Whatever I can believe, I can achieve. It's up to me to take the steps to make things happen.

Having a wealthy mindset will require you to speak right, and the belief will follow it and you will have what you say.

WHAT WE BELIEVE WE SEE

When we say something repeatedly with emotion it becomes a belief. Our mind does not care if the thoughts we are saying are true or false, therefore we can choose what thoughts to plant in our mind, which will subsequently become the words we say out of our mouths and ultimately what we believe.

I asked my daughter Jordan what she wanted to do for her 21st birthday, she replied, "I want to go skydiving." I always had the desire to experience scuba diving, white water rafting and skydiving. In my twenties I had gone scuba diving and whitewater rafting, but the opportunity had never presented itself to skydive. I agreed to honor my daughter's birthday wish. Within sixty days we were fourteen thousand feet in the air, standing in the door of an aircraft, looking down at the clouds, and we launched into the air. For about 10 minutes it was the most blissful exciting feeling ever.

Twenty years prior, I had thought about skydiving and yet had not ventured to do it. The thought had left my mind until my daughter brought it up again. Out of your subconscious your mouth utters. As I began to think about it more and more, we talked about it more and I recalled I had heard there was a place about 75 miles from my house in Mississippi that had been there for years that you could go and have this experience, and we did.

"A good man out of the good treasure of his heart bringeth forth that which is good; and an evil man out of the evil treasure of his heart bringeth forth that which is evil: for of the abundance of the heart his mouth speaketh." Luke 6:45

We should be confessing over and over again with passion what we want to come to pass in our lives. There's nothing like the power of the universe. True wealth really does begin in the mind. It's living your life on purpose and never giving up.

You must somehow trust and believe your turn will come and you will eventually see what you are believing.

WHAT WE SAY WE WILL EVENTUALLY CREATE

I started out in financial services 34 years ago. After about 90 days of being in business, I started saying, "I'm going to be a successful businessman."

I was sitting on the front row of the Doubletree Hotel at the foot of Canal Street, with a prayer in my heart: *Lord, if you bless me to become a Regional Vice President, I will bless your people.* I found something I loved to do, and I felt gratified in it. Seven months later the circumstances, conditions and opportunities presented themselves and I became a Regional Vice President. I can remember the ceremony like it was yesterday. Amazing leaders were in attendance that night: Bill Whittle, Chuck Gunnell, Francis Warren, David Landrum and thousands of others there to witness what I felt like was ordained just for me.

We are always thinking. It has been said that we think some sixty to seventy thousand thoughts a day. The problem is that 90% of those thoughts are the same thoughts we had the day before, old thoughts, old ideas, and old news. Often people's thoughts are negative rather than positive. Speaking negative words creates negative beliefs and yields negative results.

Joshua Thomas—JT, we call him—is my son and one of the future millennial Regional Vice Presidents in the Circle of Champions. A year ago, he was getting prepared to go to the African American Leadership Council (AALC) securities boot camp where he would be gone for one week. I knew the discipline and commitment to study it would take for him to prepare and grow his securities business. This license is a requirement and will help propel him to the next promotional milestone. He would really need to focus and be studious. I asked him, "Son, do you have your iPad?" He said no. He further explained that because of the inconvenience of transporting the device through airport security he would not be bringing it on the trip. I immediately realized that my son was having the wrong thoughts and took this opportunity to coach my young leader and correct his thought process.

I explained to him that along any success journey there will be minor inconveniences and your ability to solve problems and even be inconvenienced from time to time would ultimately determine how far up the success ladder you climb. The iPad would allow him the ability to access data and take notes. The minor inconvenience of airport security having him remove the device from his backpack was miniscule in proportion to the return he would receive from being adequately prepared. It's all in how we think about things—negatively or positively.

In 2000 Columbus Pollard, one of my best friends, came to town to host an event for me. He was talking about his "Vision 2007." I realized I did not have a vision like that. I immediately put pen to paper documenting where I was in my business, which was a Senior Vice President. I further charted a course to become a National Sales Director and promote 10 Regional Vice Presidents.

I changed my voicemail to announce, "You have reached the voicemail of National Sales Director, Sedrick T. Thomas." When asked what was happening, instead of saying nothing, I would reply, "We're multiplying." I changed my nameplate on my desk to National Sales Director. It could boldly be seen on my desk at entry to my office. There were mixed feelings from some people with this type of forward thinking, but it did not deter me one bit.

I began to meditate and visualize this milestone. In 2005 Hurricane Katrina struck our city and I lost the document. In 2014, while I was unpacking a box after moving into a new office (as fate would have it), the document appeared after nine years. I realized that ninety percent of the things I wrote down had come to pass. Not only was I a National Sales Director, I had promoted 16 Regional Vice Presidents and surpassed the income goal I set, and it all started with a thought planted by Columbus Pollard in 2000.

Exercising has been a lifestyle of mine for many years, and I haven't eaten meat for the past five and a half years. Having a desire to take my physical fitness to an ultimate level, I contacted my friend who is a triathlete and began to train with him. I called Roland and told him I wanted to do what it took to be a triathlete. When I met with him, he instructed me to go buy a bike. I had to go to a bike shop and spend a thousand dollars on a real bike. I had to also learn how to swim very well. Roland inspired me to do something I had never done before, enter a duathlon competition. This would require cycling and running.

It took me two hours and 14 minutes to run four miles, bike 19 miles and run four miles again, where I earned first place in my age group.

"We are what our thoughts have made us, so take care about what you think. Words are secondary. Thoughts live; they travel far."
Swami Vivekananda

ALWAYS THINK ABOUT WHAT YOU ARE THINKING ABOUT

There are three things that create our reality:

1. Thoughts we have
2. Words we speak
3. Actions that we take

Today my role is not only a businessman but coach and mentor. The people around me, like my family, teammates and friends, are all influenced by the commitment I made to invest in a lifestyle of positivity and right thinking and even more creative thinking. What you're thinking about is what you will eventually manifest in your life. In life there are no such things as coincidences.

The joy of achievement that started with a desire in my heart and having it fulfilled was everything to me. In high school I had the thought to become a successful businessman and now I am currently a National Sales Director and leader of a team of 22 businessmen and women at the Regional Vice President level that I have given the opportunity to experience the same sense of accomplishment and lifestyle I enjoy. Today I lead an organization that has over 400 individuals, with 17 of them earning incomes from $50,000-$500,000 annually.

Today I am believing for Senior National Sales Director and becoming a million-dollar income earner with my firm. Another future goal is to author a book called *The God System: Eight keys to creating and manifesting whatever you want in your life.*

If you realized just how powerful your thoughts are, you would eliminate all negative, limiting thinking.

"Nurture your mind with great thoughts, for you will never go any higher than you think." Benjamin Disraeli

True wealth begins in your mind, and your awareness of what you think about will create beliefs you will eventually get to see. Every moment, every hour, and every second of every day, we are creating what we think about. Choose those thoughts wisely.

If you are willing to do only what's easy, life will be hard. But if you are willing to do what's hard, life will be easy

T. HARV EKER

 **Terrill Knighton** is a business life coach, speaker, Master Practitioner of NLP (Nero-Linguistic Programming) and NLP Trainer.

He is the owner of NEXLVL NLP Empowerment. Terrill is a Senior Vice President with the largest marketing financial services firm in North America.

He has been a successful business owner for 27 years. His passion is to empower people with change through NLP and other self-development technologies.

Terrill has been married to Anna Knighton for over 19 years and they have four wonder children.

TERRILL KNIGHTON

When you get Better, IT Gets Better

When I was a kid, I used to watch a TV show called *Lifestyles of the Rich and Famous*. I saw people living an amazing life, and even as a 10-year-old kid, I knew that I wanted to be rich. I knew that I wanted to be successful. I remember asking my mother once if we were rich. At the time, my mother was making $12,000 a year. She said, "We're not rich, we're poor." My smile turned into a sad face. And she said, "No, no, no, no. We're not poor. We're like a lower middle class." My smile began to reverse.

The most successful person in my family was my Uncle Stan. He was an attorney. He was the only person that I really saw that was successful. He wore nice suits, drove a Mercedes, and wore too much cologne. I said, "When I grow up, I want to be a lawyer." It's not that I wanted to be a lawyer, but that was the only example of success that I saw. I knew in order to be successful you had to go to college.

So when I graduated from high school, I went straight to college. No one bought one book for me or paid for one credit hour. Yet I was totally enamored with college. I was sold out to it. I worked hard at it, waiting tables and working my way through school.

One day a gentleman came into my restaurant. He was 25 and I was only 21 at the time. He drove a luxury top-of-the-line Mercedes Benz. Today it would be the equivalent of an S550. He talked to me about the benefits of being an entrepreneur. He said, "Terrill, the man that knows how will always have a job. But the man that knows why will always be his boss. You've got to be your own boss. You've got to get into business for yourself."

I partnered with him and went into the sales profession. We were selling insurance at the time. I became a student of the entire process of sales, because selling in and of itself is a profession. I partnered with the greatest sales trainer of all time, Tom Hopkins. He's a legendary sales trainer, and I began immersing myself into the knowledge of how to sell and the profession of selling. In the process of doing that, I received schooling and training which I have applied in both my personal and professional life.

I continued to train over the years and have attended Tom Hopkins' seminar nine different times. As a result, I have become a sales professional. Two years and three months later I went completely full time in the profession of selling, and I've never looked back.

Learning a skill such as selling was about me getting better. I honed that skill in order to get better. As my results improved, my income did as well. After being a successful salesperson for approximately eight years, I added another component to my success, which was to learn how to recruit people.

While listening to a tape, I discovered the necessity of learning how to recruit. I made a total commitment to learn everything I could learn about the process of recruiting people. I was able to transform my business from one that was recruiting less than one person a month to a business that was recruiting hundreds of people a year. That launched me into a multiple six-figure income, and I've never looked back.

Over the course of my professional career, I've always sought ways to get better. I began building my own personal library with books like *Think and Grow Rich*, *How to Win Friends and Influence People*, etc.

I've read many books on success and apply the principles contained in them to my life. I have been able to build a successful business in sales, with over 500 agents and eight different offices comprising my business. I've been able earn a multiple six-figure income per year. It all stems from self-development and acquiring knowledge. Getting the necessary training for me to take myself to another level has been the catalyst for my success

I have sought out mentors and aligned myself with people that have higher-level thinking than I possessed. I believe that you need not be the smartest guy in your circle; instead, you should be the least smart guy in the circle. If you're the smartest guy in your circle, you need a new circle in order to keep improving yourself. I have always surrounded myself with business people, with people that are doing better than I am, so that I don't grow complacent and rest on my laurels. I endeavor to focus on what I need to do to move up.

I have a friend that will make a million dollars this year. I have friends that are doing very well. I surround myself intentionally with people that are doing better than I'm doing. That continues to push me and causes me to grow.

·

I continue to acquire professional sales skills and training. I realized after reading a book titled *Think and Grow Rich* that your thought process has everything to do with your success. Where you are in life right now is a sum total of your thoughts. For your life to get better, your thinking must get better.

Your best thinking has gotten you to where you are in life right now. I came across a concept called NLP, or Neuro Linguistic Programing. NLP is the practice of understanding how people organize their thinking, feeling, language, and behavior to produce their results. NLP provides people with the methodology to model outstanding performances achieved by leaders in their field. It's also used for personal development and success in business.

When I came across this concept, I realized that it gave me an opportunity to model what other people do—in essence to model their success. Not just their behavior, but also the way that they think. I internalized that concept and became a master practitioner. The strategies of NLP allowed me to continue my success and move forward.

A concept that helped me tremendously is understanding we have two distinct minds. We have a conscious mind, which we use to think with. We also have our subconscious mind, which comprises 95% of our mind. Our conscious mind is the other 5%. This led to the understanding that most of our life is on autopilot. You're not consciously aware of why you do all the things you do because the things you're doing stem from your subconscious.

Look at it like this: your mind is like a ship. Your conscious mind is the bridge. It's at the top and your subconscious mind is below the water line. It's in the engine room. When the captain of the ship says, "More power; increase the speed of the engine," the guy in the engine room does exactly what the captain says. He doesn't have the capability to say yes or no. That's the way your subconscious mind works.

Your conscious mind sends messages down to your subconscious mind. Regardless of whether those messages are good or bad, the subconscious mind will act upon them without thinking. Over the years, after conditioning and how we grow up, our subconscious mind begins to take in all types of messages. It begins to drive our behavior and we often are unconscious of where those directives come from.

One thing that is imperative is to understand the power of the mind, and how our mind works in the first place. When you begin to understand that, you can have a greater impact on becoming successful. You can become a lot more intentional, rather than just being on autopilot and not really understanding why you do the things you do. Understanding the power of the mind, understanding how your subconscious and your conscious mind are tied together, will allow you to be successful.

We think 60-70,000 thoughts every single day. The challenge is, 90% of those thoughts are the same thoughts that we had from the day before. We keep thinking the same thing, we keep doing the same thing, and we keep getting the same thing. Then we say, "My life's not changing!"

For your life to change, you're going to have to change what you're thinking. You must do what is called Meta – Cognition. You must think about what you're thinking about. I don't know if you've ever taken the time to do that, but if you take the time to think about what you're thinking about, you might be surprised at what you're thinking about!

When you can become aware of the direction of your thoughts, then you can begin to change them. But you can't change them until you become aware of them. Thoughts that are emotionalized become magnetized and attract similar and alike thoughts. This is called the law of attraction.

We emotionalize and we think about all kinds of things. We think and emotionalize good things, and we think and emotionalize things that are not so good. Either way, we attract everything that's in our life. We are creating our own life, based on our thoughts. At the end of the day, you're going to become what you think about. Your mind is a sending and receiving station for the vibrations of thought.

When you think about things, you put those thoughts in the universe. It's like when you think about somebody and then a few minutes later they call you on the phone. That happens often with people. They say, "WOW, I was just thinking about you." Well, you put that thought in the universe. You put it out there and as a result that thought created that result.

You must become consciously aware of how you're thinking, and you must become intentional about what you want to think. You must tell yourself another story. We're always telling ourselves stories. We're telling ourselves empowering stories, or we're telling ourselves stories that are disempowering.

I have found that by using four simple steps you can get Better and make IT get Better. The person who makes up their mind to implement and employ the four simple steps will see significant increase in Impact, Influence and Income. The four simple steps are:

STEP 1: DO A META-COGNITIVE (THINK ABOUT WHAT YOU ARE THINKING ABOUT)

To change the direction of your life, you want to tell yourself a different story. You want to create the story of success. You want to create the story that you want to manifest in your life. Often, we have negative thoughts in the back of our mind. We have self-doubts and limiting beliefs. The way to counteract those self-defeating thoughts and limiting beliefs is to create a whole new story and begin to meditate on that story and tell yourself that story over and over repeatedly. In other words, rewrite the program.

If you feel like you're getting older, you tell yourself the story: I'm getting better, I'm more refined, and these are my best years. Rather than saying I'm getting old, my body is breaking down, and I'm probably going to get sick, you tell yourself the story: These are going to be my best years. I'm going to be in optimal health and I'm going to be better than ever. You make the decision to tell yourself that story versus letting the negative thoughts and limiting beliefs creep in and tell you that you're about to get sick, or when people get older, they can't move around as well—that type of thing.

The reason you've been stuck is because of what you've been thinking. You must to get past that type of thinking. Once you get past that thinking, you will start to get and become better. That's why I always say, "When you get better, IT gets better." The way you get better is to continue empowering yourself with new thoughts, a new story, a new intention so that you can get to that new place where you want to be.

That change that one needs to do is called Meta-Cognition. What that means is you must take the time to think about what you're thinking about, to observe your thoughts, and when you do, you might be surprised to realize what you've been thinking. Often you are focused on a lot of doubt; you've been having a lot of limited beliefs. Even though you're saying with your mouth that you want one thing, your thoughts may not be in alignment with what you say you want. Meta-Cognition gives you a chance to just think about what you think about and observe your own thoughts.

We go through life in a routine, running on autopilot because we've been driven by our subconscious and we become unconscious of our own thoughts. When you get in your car to turn the keys, you just go. I remember one day I was going to go home and park in the front of my house; the next thing I knew, I was pulling in the back of the house in the garage because I was on autopilot. We must take the time to think about what we're thinking about.

STEP 2: DECIDE WHAT YOU WANT

Decide what you want. That's a big win. Taking the time to really think about what you want is not as easy as it sounds. It seems easy but if you take the time to really think about what you want; you must get clear on what it is that you want. You must take the time to really decide what it is that you want.

STEP 3: CREATE A NEW STORY

You must have clarity on that goal you want to accomplish in your life. You must write it down. You must put it on paper. You've got to physically write it down on paper so that it's intentional; you must put it in writing. Once you've got it in writing there is power. There is accountability in writing down your goals. That accountability mandates that they will come into fruition. They come together when you put it down on paper.

You need to tell yourself the story of how you're going to come up with everything in life you want. You need to tell yourself your story all day long. You've got to tell yourself your story when you wake up and before you go to bed. For example, the story goes like this:

"I'm going to have an incredible year this year. I'm going to reach all my goals. I'm going to receive everything I want. I'm going to be to be healthy. I'm going to always be prospering"

Tell yourself that story when you wait in line at the bank; tell yourself your story when you're stuck in traffic. Just rewrite the program, write over top of the negative program and create a beautiful story of the life you want to create.

STEP 4: MEDITATE

Think about it and meditate on it every single day. I suggest 15 minutes a day, perhaps in the morning or perhaps before you go to bed, but you must spend 15 minutes getting quiet and thinking about, meditating on, your golden dreams. In doing so you're going to change your life, goals and dreams, and create the life you dreamed of.

If you make a point of doing these four steps intentionally you will begin to see the changes in life you have always desired and dreamed of. Life is lived in a negative environment for so many people for so long that it has begun to seem normal. These principles and techniques are designed to make you conscious and aware of your surroundings and your thoughts. Once you have control of those elements in your life, you will indeed be better, and IT will without question Get Better!

Mike and Regina Evans

Michael J. Evans is a Leader of Leaders. A Servant, Teacher, Lecturer, Life Coach, Financial Planner, Recruiter & Business Owner. He has been a servant in ministry and a business owner for more than 30 years. Mike is a product of the Chicago Public School System having graduated from Calumet High School on the south side of Chicago. He is also a graduate of Northern Illinois University, with a BA Degree. While at Northern he was elected Treasurer of the Student Association, where he oversaw over $600,000 of student activity fees. He also became a member of Phi Beta Sigma Fraternity.

Mike is a Senior National Sales Director for a NYSE Company. He has over 30 years of experience in financial services and has built an organization of more than 1,900 personal financial analysts whose total focus is "helping families earn income, protect their income, eliminate debt, and accumulate wealth." He has 46 franchise owners across 12 states, with plans to open 50 additional offices in the next 5 years. He has built No. 1 agencies in both Illinois and Indiana and has received the prestigious MVP Award from his company. Mike, along with his wife Regina, was featured in USA Today, February 2019, as one of the top business owners within his company. He is currently expanding his organization for individuals that he will train and develop to own their own franchises. His personal philosophy is simple: God 1st, family 2nd, and business 3rd.

Mike Evans and his wife, Regina, have been married more than 30 years and are proud parents and grandparents. He says that his family is his greatest responsibility.

Regina Evans is a native of the south side of Chicago. She began her study of both semi-professional and professional dance at a very young age at the Sammy Dyer School of the Theatre and Shirley Hall Bass Modern Dance Company. Regina was the first African

American female that received a BA degree in Theatre Dance from Northern Illinois University. She is a member of Delta Sigma Theta. Regina has worked side by side with her husband Michael in the financial Services Industry for over 30 years helping to develop, train and mentor hundreds of Leaders to become successful Entrepreneurs as well as empowering families to take control of their financial future.

It's easier to stand on the

sidelines, criticize, and say

why you shouldn't do something.

The sidelines are crowded.

Get in the game.

ROBERT KIYOSAKI

Mike & Regina Evans

Are You The One or Shall I Look for Another One?

I was born in the inner-city projects of Chicago. I experienced a great deal of adversity as a young child growing up. With all the negative things that I experienced and faced being raised in the projects, dreaming became a regular event for me to escape the realities around me. I can remember often dreaming about being a millionaire, living in a mansion and owning multiple properties. This reminds me of the words written by Harriet Tubman: "Every great dream begins with a great dreamer. Always remember, you have within you the strength, the patience and the passion to reach for the stars to change the world." My mother made me memorize famous Black poems that I had to recite to her often. The one thing that my mother embedded in my mind the most, especially when I half-did a task, is the anonymous quote, "Once a task has begun never leave it till it's done. Be the labor big or small, do it well or not at all."

During this same time in St. Louis, Missouri a young woman had given birth to her firstborn son. She was heavily influenced by the TV series *Dallas*. It kept her focused on the declaration she'd made over her son years ago that he would be the first millionaire in their family.

Later in life these two individuals would meet at a college university, date, eventually get married and start a family. Was this union simply a coincidence or was it fate? After college we both began our separate careers. I was a dance teacher and choreographer at The Chicago Academy for The Arts High School and Michael worked for Sunstrand Corporation in Rockford, Illinois as a contract negotiator. I was the mental thinker, the processor, the structured, creative, and visual planner. Michael was the action-oriented doer, the let's-get-it-done-now, friendly people person with the gift of public speaking. What's so funny about this scenario is that as a child, Michael had a tied tongue. The doctors told his mother that he would need to have his tongue clipped because he would not be able to talk. Ha! Michael speaks very well. He is a natural born speaker.

There is a very specific reason we titled this chapter "Are You The One or Shall I Look for Another One?"

PHG... Praise, Honor and Glory. Just as my wife did, I'd like to also give just a little of my background. My name is Michael J. Evans. I'm from St. Louis, Missouri originally and our family moved to Chicago when I was in the eighth grade. I graduated from Calumet High School, on the South Side of Chicago, and completed my education with a Bachelor's degree at Northern Illinois University in Dekalb. That's where I met my beautiful Delta Sigma Theta girlfriend, and now wife, Regina. While at Northern I was elected Treasurer of the Student Association, where I oversaw over $600,000 of student activity fees. In my Sophomore year I pledged and became a member of Phi Beta Sigma Fraternity. Also, during my time at Northern I met a gentleman by the name of McKinley Deacon Davis, who became my mentor, and to this day I'm still grateful to him and his wife Lil. McKinley passed away in March of 2003, but the impact he had on my life and so many others will live forever.

Once I graduated from Northern (after five years and a summer) I got my first job as a contract negotiator for an aviation company that sold parts for the B1 Bomber MX missile, space shuttle and civilian aircrafts. I remember shortly after being hired at this company Human Resources asked all new employees to complete the paperwork for our 401(k) plans. No one had ever talked to me about putting together a 401(k) plan. I had no idea what I was doing or how to do it. I saw other people in the room typing and clicking on the computer, and they seemed to be very knowledgeable when it came to their investment options. So I just acted like I knew what I was doing and typed and clicked as well, not having any idea what I was doing. I was so confused and embarrassed that I did not know which options to select or how to set up my 401(k) plan for retirement.

A few months after I began working, I bumped into Deacon Davis. It had been a little while since I'd seen him. He told me about a company he was involved in that I needed to consider working with. However, I felt the timing wasn't right, so I did not take advantage of the opportunity. Although I declined taking a look at the opportunity Deacon must have seen something in me because more than a year later, he got in contact with me again. Deacon talked to me once more about coming on board to work with him, and I made the decision to do just that. That decision changed my entire life and how I think about wealth. That's how I came to know that wealth starts in the mind, because of the seeds of knowledge he planted in me regarding how money works.

I'd like to share a story I once heard about three people who were flying on a private jet... a preacher, a professor and a Boy Scout. Things were going smoothly until suddenly the pilot came running out of the cockpit and told all three people that there was a problem with the engine and the plane was going down. The pilot quickly explained that there were only three parachutes, then he took one, strapped it on and jumped. The professor looked at the preacher and the Boy Scout and said, "I'm the smartest man in the world. I'm going to have to take this parachute because the world is going to need me." He strapped on the second parachute and jumped. The Boy Scout and the preacher were standing there looking at one other when the Boy Scout told the preacher, "We're going to be OK." The preacher responded, "No son, we're not. The plane is going down. But since there's only one parachute left you need to take it because I already know how I'm going to spend eternity." The little boy insisted, "No, we're going to be OK, we're gonna be OK!" And the preacher said, "No, we're not. Why do you keep thinking we're going to be OK when there's only one parachute left?" Then the Boy Scout responded, "We still have two parachutes left because the smartest man in the world just jumped off the plane with my book bag!"

The moral of the story is you don't have to be the smartest person in the world to understand how to play the money game. I've learned how to win when it comes to money, and I teach others every day. And I hope that you learn something through this book that will teach you the same thing because true wealth starts in the mind.

I remember Deacon meeting with Regina and me one night and putting together a financial game plan, which we now call a Financial Needs Analysis, to help us get on track financially. We were both 26 at the time. I was always raised to give the first 10% of my income for tithes. But Deacon also talked to us about paying ourselves as well. He used the term 10 / 10 / 80, which represents paying 10% in tithes, 10% to yourself (savings) and living off the remaining 80%. I remember him teaching us about mutual funds, how to bypass the middleman and the Rule of 72 (that calculates how long it takes your money to double) which I had never heard of. He also taught Regina and me about debt stacking, which showed us how to eliminate the debt that we had sooner, and how to protect my income so that when I die my family will still be able to survive and have a legacy, because my income will still keep coming in. I remember very clearly, like it was yesterday, going back to work to speak to a friend who worked side-by-side with me for three years, and saying to him, "I have something to tell you!" I was so excited about telling him what I'd learned. He kept asking, "What is it, what is it?" And I said, "I can't tell you right now because if I tell you right now you might start shouting and running all around the office." So when we took our break and he kept asking what I had to tell him I said, "I just found out that you can get a mutual fund started that can probably pay you 6, 8, 10 or 12% and you can get started with as little as $25 a month!" He said, "I know that's not what you had to tell me." When I said yes, that was it, he looked at me as though I said you can get a checkbook with carbon on the back, which everybody knows these days. He couldn't believe that's what I wanted to tell him. After he stopped laughing, I asked him why he was laughing like that. He said, "Mike, I thought everybody knew about mutual funds. My parents opened my first mutual fund for me when I was in the third grade." I couldn't believe he said that. I thought he was my friend. I asked why he'd never shared this information with me. He looked me in my eyes, and I believed him with all my heart when he said to me, "Mike, I thought everybody knew about mutual funds." But I did not.

When we received our completed financial plan, Deacon suggested that we set up three different accounts... one would be for emergencies, the second was a short-term fund and the third one was a long-term fund for my retirement. He gave each of us a risk profile questionnaire and asked several questions to help determine how aggressive or conservative each of us would be when it came to our investments. It was at that point I gained a full understanding of what I needed to do to set up my 401(k) Retirement Plan. If more people had this information and understood it, they would do a better job of allocating the funds with clarity and confidence.

My mother once shared with me that she used to watch a TV show that aired from 1955-1960 called *The Millionaire*. It centered around a gentleman named Michael Anthony who sought out struggling individuals to deliver $1 million checks to on behalf of his employer. It was this show that inspired her to name my brother and me Anthony and Michael, respectively, even before we were born, with the belief that we would one day become millionaires and be able to help others attain wealth.

One day, several years ago, I went to my mom's house early in the morning to pick something up. I had been in the business for a few years at that point. She said, "Mike, come here, I have a question for you." Then she told me before she asked me the question, she wanted me to look in the mirror, because she wanted me to be looking at myself when I answered her question. She prayed over us regularly and was always very deep with teaching us about life, so I wasn't sure where she was going with this question that morning. She asked if I was ready and I said yes. She then told me to look into the mirror. The question she asked was "Are you the one or shall I look for another one?" In my mind I was repeating what she said... *Are you the one or shall I look for another one?* I wasn't clear at first. She told me to answer the question, yes or no. I asked her what she meant. She said, "Michael, are you going to be the one who makes sure your family does not go through another broke generation? Are you going to be the one who makes sure the children in this family who want and need to go to college can still have a shot at going college without worrying about money? Are you going to be the one to help me through retirement? Are you going to be the one who makes $1 million a year at some point in your life?"

My mother was so deep. I looked in the mirror after listening and
thinking about what she just asked me. I said yes. "Yes, I will be
the one and you don't have to look for another one." It was at that
moment that I stepped out on faith and asked God to lead and guide
me, and he has done just that. After I came to myself, I asked my
mother where she got that question. She said she didn't know, it just
dropped in her spirit. So I asked again, thinking it had to come from
somewhere. She thought for a while and she said "You know what? I
think it came from a movie I was watching last night." When I asked
what movie, she said *The Matrix*. She reminded me that in the movie
Morpheus kept wanting to ask Neo if he was The One or should they
look for another One. Neo didn't know he was The One. Morpheus
began to tell Neo why it was that he believed he was The One, and
Neo was blown away with the explanation Morpheus gave him.

Neo is offered the choice between the Blue Pill and continuing to
live in a synthesized, fictional, computer-generated world, or taking
the Red Pill and joining the real world and escape from the Matrix:
"You take the blue pill...the story ends, you wake up in your bed
and believe whatever you want to believe. You take the red pill...you
stay in Wonderland...and I show you how deep the rabbit hole goes.
Remember. . . all I'm offering is the truth." *

Neo decided he was going to take the red pill because he wanted freedom for everyone. However, Neo still wasn't certain that he was The
One until he got into a fight and some men began shooting at him.
He began to move as fast as lightning, dodging all the bullets that
came at him. At one point he felt the special power that came with
being The One. As the other men continued shooting Neo raised his
hand straight out in front of him and all the bullets stopped in front
of his hand and fell to the ground. It was at that very moment Neo
knew he was The One.

As she began to tell me that story it made me think about another story that came from the greatest book ever written in the world… the Bible. In Luke chapter 7, verses 18 through 22, John the Baptist was about to be beheaded and he sent two of the disciples to go find this man named Jesus. As the story goes:

¹⁸ Then the disciples of John reported to him concerning all these things.

¹⁹ And John, calling two of his disciples to him, sent them to Jesus, saying, "Are You the Coming One, or do we look for another?"

²⁰ When the men had come to Him, they said, "John the Baptist has sent us to You, saying, 'Are You the Coming One, or do we look for another?'"

²¹ And that very hour He cured many of infirmities, afflictions, and evil spirits; and to many blind He gave sight.

²² Jesus answered and said to them, "Go and tell John the things you have seen and heard: that the blind see, the lame walk, the lepers are cleansed, the deaf hear, the dead are raised, the poor have the gospel preached to them…."

So now my question to you is are you going to be the one or will your family have to look for another one? I believe after reading this book you will be empowered to know that you were pre-destined to be the one that's going to take the time to study to show yourself approved. There's a saying that reads "When the student is ready the teacher will appear." I challenge that you will submit yourself to being coach-able and be mentored by someone who can help you grow and reach your full potential. You will partner with a financial coach who can lead you where you need to go to make sure your family does not go through another broke generation, who can show you how to position yourself to be the lender and not the borrower.

Together we begin the journey that put us on the path for success. When you follow the path that God has planned for you and surrender totally to the journey, despite the odds, setbacks, failures and challenges of life, God will bless you in ways that you cannot imagine. Do not be afraid! Remember, there is power in repetition and simplicity. The test is to remain humble, steadfast and prayerful.

For all that we have, and all that we are, glory be to God. The Lord has allowed me to be the one for my family, and my mother does not have to look for another. Regina and I count it an honor and a blessing to be an example for not only our family, but for so many others. To not only be able to have the understanding that true wealth starts in the mind but to also understand the importance of empowering others with this information is a humbling experience. I want you to go forth and challenge yourself to be your very best and seek out the information you need so that you can also be the one for your family. Live each day with love, gratitude and praise.

PHG... Praise, Honor and Glory. See you at the top.

*From the film *The Matrix*, a Warner Bros. production

 **Chauvon Landry** was born and raised in Hollygrove in New Orleans, Louisiana. She began her career at a very young age as a local entertainer, nabbing roles in local videos, movies and winning rap battles around the city. Her star rose quickly as a rapper but soon after, she became a single mother and decided to reevaluate her career.

Chauvon made the decision to become a financial advisor and learn a field she had no experience in. She worked double shifts as a waitress while building the business. As a result, she took the same work ethic and hustle that launched her entertainment career and cultivated a half million-dollar financial firm with her business partner and husband Antoine Landry. The company has 5 locations, 13 vice presidents and 250 agents. She is now the mother of 4 children with very active schedules all while traveling around the country twice a month as a motivational speaker and entrepreneurial business expert. She and her husband are also the owners of Beastnation Enterprises Inc. She also leads the PINK BEAST MOVEMENT and hosts multiple women's empowerment events throughout the year. She is passionate about leading all women, yet she specifically targets single mothers and teaches them that if she can do it so can they. Chauvon has a simple yet effective motto in life, "You don't get paid to feel, you get paid to finish".

CHAUVON LANDRY
If I Had Known Then What I Know Now

How often do we say to ourselves, "I wish I had known that before?" If I could just take today's wisdom and give it to the single mom in me who started building a business ten years ago, man, to think of HOW MUCH BIGGER I WOULD BE TODAY! HOW MANY MORE LIVES COULD I HAVE IMPACTED BY NOW? Would I have struggled for as long as I did? If I had known what I know now, would I still have needed to get extensions on those bills? Would I still have cried those tears wondering if I would be able to give my baby the life she deserved? The answer is…probably not. At the same time, if I had not gone through those character-building, faith-strengthening, trying times, would I have worked as hard to change my situation? Would I have ever learned how resilient I truly was? Would I be able to say that I know firsthand and have experienced the power of God? Those answers are also… probably not. Was I raised with a silver spoon and everything handed to me? Nope! But now that I know what I know about life and the fact that I had to work for everything I have today, I know in my heart that it is what made me a BEAST!

Today, ten years later, my husband and I lead a team of over 300 people, across six states. I often sit at my desk and smirk to myself wondering where all this wisdom was when I needed it. Now, I mentor my Regional Vice Presidents with hopes that I can help them avoid making the same mistakes I did. But let's go back for a second...

In December 2009, I stepped out on faith into the world of entrepreneurship without a clue about the leader I would need to grow into to be able to build a successful empire. I met my husband in the same financial services industry I was in and we decided to merge businesses and open our own franchise together. That's where it all began! I figured we would simply teach people financial concepts and fundamentals to building and we'd build our business toward success. It sounded simple enough; this should be a breeze. But I soon found out most people don't struggle with learning basic skills—they struggle with being able to apply what they've been taught when they're facing adversity. Honestly, I think we've all been guilty of this at some point in our lives. I've been taught to always "think positive" and I know I've been taught to "speak positively." But in the face of adversity, is that really doable? OF COURSE, IT IS! It is not always easy to do but it is ALWAYS doable and your reward for choosing to do it is definitely worth it.

When the retention of our people starts to decline, I can't help but wonder why they weren't tough enough to stay the course. I understand that rejection can sometimes hurt people, but why did it kill them? I get it—adversity in life and business is challenging, but why did it bury them? I wasn't confused about why these things slowed them down because we've all been hit, thrown off guard and slowed down before. Still, I was completely perplexed about why they allowed these things, people or situations to bring them to a complete halt in their business. I became intrigued with this rationale and began to search for data that could give me insight on the difference between the weak and the strong. Finally, I reached somewhat of a broad conclusion: IT WAS MENTAL TOUGHNESS! But could these two words, this one concept, really have that much impact? They definitely did!

The more I researched, the more I understood. It was really surprising for me when I discovered women tend to struggle with mental toughness most. I had to find out WHY? I mean, after all, women are the best multi-taskers ever, right? We cook, clean, raise kids, take care of our husbands, work, hit our goals, keep the home environment up to par, etc., and the fact that we maintain our sanity through it all is impressive, I must say. But the more I researched, the more it was clear that the reasoning behind women's struggles with mental toughness is that we are emotional creatures.

But what does that mean, exactly— "emotional?" I started questioning myself: "Are you emotional, Chauvon? Do your emotions put you in a positive place to win? Or are they the reason you slow down?" The more I reflected, the more I realized it wasn't simply "emotions" that slowed us down, it was our EMOTIONAL DECISION MAKING. That day I decided, since emotions are immature (because they change like the weather), then they should not have such a significant role in my life and decision making. But was that enough? If I taught this concept to the women at our headquarters, would it be enough? Would that prevent them from making the emotional decision to quit just because they had a bad day, bad week, or even a bad month? Would that prevent them from making the emotional decision to shy away from the sales strategies we taught them just to avoid rejection? If so, I'd be willing to give it a try. I mean, after all, what do I have to lose? Nothing. But, if this is actually going to be a game-changing intervention, then I have everything to gain! The optimistic thought of "gain" drove me to becoming obsessed with developing the blueprint of the ideal business mind of a woman.

I was obsessed with not being the average woman with average thinking. But I was even more obsessed with instilling that same obsession into the women I was training and mentoring. I was determined to learn as much as possible to put the odds in my favor. I wanted to ensure that, whenever I'm training or mentoring a woman in business, I could know sooner than later if she lacked mental toughness. Although we spent time teaching our team financial principles, we spent more time teaching mental toughness. It was crucial that people learned how to turn lemons into lemonade and to turn lemonade into lemon stands! If we were going to build a huge empire that we wanted to last in our family for generations and generations, then we had to either find or build people with mental toughness.

So here I am today, after reading books, listening to audios and studying biographies of enormously successful people, and I now realize that there is no better source in the world that would give me more data and information than experience herself. After experiencing years of training and mentoring women in business with different personality types, I've developed my own synopsis. I believe if a woman truly has a desire to win big in business and to stay the course, there are certain things she must learn to do and not to do. With the burning desire to increase the number of people we retained in this business; I was not going to stop until I figured out what those things were. I have a better idea of what those things are now than I did when I first started years ago. My mindset had to shift if I was serious about gaining wealth in this industry. Here's what I've learned: A woman must be extremely mentally tough to overcome the distractions that come her way daily. This requires her to choose to be resilient—notice I said *choose* to be. Resilience is a choice. Choosing to not stay down even when life knocks you down is a choice. It is a tough choice, but tough choices yield the biggest rewards. From there, I narrowed it down to three abilities that we must have to win big. As soon as I narrowed it down, I began to add it into our weekly team trainings. I believe the people who develop these three abilities will be the people who can beat the odds against all things that were meant to stop them in their tracks toward success. As I looked back on all the ladies who didn't stay the course, I realized they didn't have these abilities. The winners, those who are experiencing high levels of success, have these three abilities. And even ME! As I reflected, I realized that I began to double and triple my income when I developed these abilities. So trust me when I tell you these three abilities WILL make a difference:

ABILITY #1: You must have the ability to go back and find the directions whenever you get lost in the business. Life sometimes hands you situations and circumstances that cause you to lose your momentum in business. Whether it is a woman having a baby or just a "down" season, we have all had times when we had to get back into the game and kick our momentum back up. When it is time to do that, you need to have the ability to find the directions. The directions can be found in the basics or in the person who created the path. By that, I mean going back to those everyday habits that you committed to when you gained your momentum before. Go back to the tools you need to get organized to strategize your win. For example, when I want to kick my momentum up, I know I need to start talking to ten people a day about my business. I know I need an appointment book that shows me my entire week so I can know and see how full or empty my week is, based on my set appointments. I need an inventory log to keep track of all the prospects that I need to call to schedule appointments with. I need a goal book to constantly write my goals down and keep them in front of me. Last, I need a tracking system so I can do an autopsy of my business by day, week and month to track my progress. The confidence I have with kicking up momentum comes from me knowing the tools that will give me direction. When you don't know what those tools are, then you need to get directions from the person who created the path. Go to your coach or mentor for advice. People often get lost and get discouraged, and then a domino effect from doubts sets in. Now they're spending all their time being lost and talking to other lost people-, and none of them have the directions. So I began teaching about the ability to find directions whenever you get lost.

ABILITY #2: You need to develop the ability to play hurt. We often hear about football and basketball players who still get in the game and score, even after they've hurt a finger, arm, leg or ankle. The champions still get in the game and play anyway. What I've learned about women is they tend to be more impacted by mental pain than they are by physical pain. A woman with a broken heart can be one of the most non-productive women you will ever meet if she isn't mentally tough enough to play hurt. Whether it is relationships, issues with your spouse, disappointment from a mentor, unmet expectations from business partners or betrayal from a friend, you must get the work done anyway. When I saw women going through these things, I observed how the world immediately counted them out. Most women are not expected to bounce back in business while simultaneously going through a heartbreak. I became obsessed with not playing the business game the way "most women" play it. I wanted the women I was training to not react like "most women" would either. I began training on the ability to play through the hurt.

ABILITY #3: You need the ability to not judge your success based on the lack of success of others. People tend to base the height of their success on others' successes or lack thereof. Because you've only seen them go so far does not mean you won't go farther. Maybe they won't build relationships like you, maybe they won't apologize like you, or forgive like you… Maybe they aren't committed like you, working through holidays and birthdays for a few years like you will... or maybe they have arrived at the level of success their heart desired. Who knows the reasoning behind why they stopped at that point? You need to believe you can be a record breaker and hit milestones that have never been hit before. I decided not to judge my success on the success of others and began to train others to do the same.

It took me some time to narrow it down but once I observed the areas where I and other women were having struggles were related to mental toughness, I was able to train on it. They learned how to prepare for these times before they reached them, so they were able to stay strong and come out of them. I think every day about how many more women I could have helped to change their lives if I had known then what I know now. But, like my Grandmother Anna always said, "It's spilled milk now; clean it up and fix another glass"—meaning you've made that mistake early, so clean it up and do it right the next time. That's what I have been doing as I continue to experience and learn more and more information that I can use to help women in business. I continue to train on being mentally tough and staying the course long enough to achieve history-making success!

 **Lee A. Williams** is an Entrepreneur, Financial Strategist, Coach, and Public Speaker. He earned his B.A. in Broadcast Journalism & Mass Communications from the University of South Carolina. He served as a previous President of the University of South Carolina Black Alumni Council.

After an eight-year career in television, Mr. Williams opened a financial services agency. He also started a Men's Ministry for colleagues in the entrepreneurial and financial services industry. Lee is an ordained deacon. He is a member of the African American Leadership Council. He also began weekly studies of the "Men's Fraternity" in local men's prisons.

Margo Williams is a Relationship & Conflict Coach, Minister, Ministry Consultant, Creative Writer, and Public Speaker. She earned her B.S. in Marketing & B.S. in Insurance and Economic Security from the University of South Carolina and her Master of Divinity from Columbia International University Seminary and School of Missions. Ms. Williams is currently a Doctoral Candidate at Erskine Theological Seminary with an emphasis on Conflict Resolution and Restoration.

Additionally, Margo directs Margo W. Williams Ministries, a registered 501 (c) 3. This ministry is dedicated to serving the needs of the family by providing conflict resolution, life skills training, assertiveness training and spiritual life enhancements.

LEE AND MARGO WILLIAMS
No More Backwards Thinking

I believe most people think backwards. They look at their physical situation, get emotional about it, then think of what to do. This is called backwards thinking. In order to stop thinking backwards and think forward, you must grow up. And growing up is a decision. We are all familiar with growing up. Physically, your body changes. Are you aware that you can grow up physically but never grow up mentally and never grow up emotionally? Mental growth is one of the keys to becoming wealthy.

I'm reminded of a story. I remember growing up in government housing in Spartanburg, South Carolina. My mother had four children. I was the second oldest. I saw my mother working two full-time jobs because she wanted to give her children a different life. She worked in cotton mills and rubber plants for years. However, in between those jobs, while changing clothes, she would say, "Son, use your head for more than just a hat rack." I would nod my head and say, "Yes ma'am." But in my mind, I was saying, *what is she talking about? Riddles, riddles, I hate Batman.*

Game Day: On this special day, I went outside, which was dangerous because there were older boys. We didn't call them 'gangs' back then, just older boys. They would beat you up if you didn't do what they said. I ran to my friend's apartment unseen by the older boys because I was fast. Later, my friend and I went outside together. He was not as fast as me, so we got caught by the older boys. One of the initiations for living in the neighborhood was if you did not want to get beat up, you had to go into the local store and steal snacks so the older boys would have something to eat. The older boys would stand behind the store and threaten you by saying, "You better get something good." We were five or six years old. My friend and I were sweating bullets. We entered the Handy Pantry. We split up. I spotted a snack and slid it into my pants pocket and walked out of the store. "What you got for us?" they shouted. I kept my hand tightly closed until they all gathered around. I threw the one piece of super bubblegum in the air and ran like the wind while they fought over who was going to get it. They yelled, "We gonna get you." *Not today,* I said to myself as I was sprinting back to my building. I rushed upstairs and went to the back window, where I had a view of the store. I saw the store manager holding my friend by the collar with one hand and a bag of potato chips in the other hand. *Chips,* I thought. *Don't they make noises when you try to put them in your pants?* The police arrived shortly and put my friend in the car. The officers drove off but turned into our neighborhood. They pulled up to the front of our building and my heart stopped as they took my friend to his mother's apartment. My mom and I watched this from the screen door. Then my mom said, "Lee, were you and your friend not together? What happened?" I replied, "I used my head for more than just a hat rack."

DECISION

Reminds me of a story about a squirrel. One day a couple and their two young children were driving home from the family vacation when the father spotted a dead squirrel in the road. He slowed the car down so his family could carefully observe the scene as he rolled by. The father, being a teacher, recognized a teachable moment. Looking at his wife beside him in the front seat, he asked, "Margo, honey, what do you think killed the squirrel?" "Teenagers driving too fast in a car," she replied. He then looked at his eight-year-old son. "Matt, what killed the squirrel?" "It was a motorcycle," he answered. Last, the father asked his precious four-year-old daughter, Morgan, "Baby girl, what do you think killed the squirrel?" "It was a big ole truck!" she shouted. After a nodding to his family as a way of saying thank you for their answers, he said, "It wasn't the teenagers, a motorcycle, or a truck that killed the squirrel. It was INDECISION. You see, the squirrel should have been across the road a long time ago if he had just made up his mind and stopped going back and forth." Indecision killed the squirrel just like it's killing your goals and dreams. Becoming wealthy is not an accident. It will only happen after you make a decision that's non-negotiable.

The longest period of time in a person's life is not the amount of time it takes to do "a thing," but it's the time that it takes to just MAKE THE DECISION.

Winners are not afraid of making decisions, even if some of them are wrong.

When the decision plate is in front of you and you don't make a decision, then that plate will be passed on to someone else and they will make a decision that might not be in your favor.

There is an order to thinking forward and not backwards. An illustration of the 3-Hs can help you understand. The proper order is head, heart and hands. Let's begin with the head. It's in your head you store the seeds of thought. You must believe that thoughts become things. It is true; your thoughts can create your reality. This is why when you have visions and dreams you should write them down. They have a 42% chance of becoming real. Only 3% of people write down their goals. You've always, always got to be in the top three. The head stores your mentality and your mindset can build or kill the greatness within.

The heart is second. In your heart is where you store your emotions, your feelings. You can learn how to properly attach the correct emotions to the right thoughts to grow greatness. You must practice. Remember, when emotions are up, intelligence is down. And when intelligence is up, emotions are down. Experts say that 5% of mankind uses intelligence to rule the 95% of the people who are emotional. The 5% create situations and circumstances knowing how the 95% will emotionally respond, which makes the end results totally predictable. You must transition from making emotional decisions to making intelligent decisions.

The hands would be last, but certainly not least. They will be doing the physical work and completing all the assignments that your head came up with and your heart has to agree to. Your hands will now perform the required action needed to complete the task.

YOUR MIND IS AN ENVIRONMENT WHERE YOU CAN CHANGE THE WORLD, one thought at a time. Let's go into the kitchen where the chef (you) prepares today's meal. On today's menu: A Winning Environment. Let's see...you will need: A cup of Exposure, a pint of Experiences, a tablespoon of Excitement (not too much now, you don't want to look like a fool). Sample it. Now the environment is almost ready. For best results repeat, repeat, repeat. So E+E+E = E. If your environment doesn't produce what you thought it should, check the cup of experience. Remember, exposure to something does not mean there was an experience of something. If YOU did all the talking and there was no participation or involvement from the other parties, you didn't teach; you told. There must be constant roleplay from different angles in order to decide on what's best and recycle the rest.

MINDSETTING

A phone and computers have settings and so does your mind. You can categorize them into three different settings: survival, success and significance.

Let's look at who plays a role in the setting of your mind. Parents play a major role in the mind-setting of their children. There are many others that play a role as well, such as peers and people in certain environments like schools, churches, clubs and sports. Your past, your problems and your performances are contributing factors as well.

Many people's minds were never set on how to build wealth. They were set on how to survive. To reset the mind, you will need new instructions on how to build a mind of wealth. It's going to require new teachers using new techniques. I'm not saying the information is new to mankind, but maybe just new to you. It is now time to 'flip the script' or if you are ready, let's 'script the flip.'

You have a voice, a pen and paper. Take the ideas, which are in your head and can easily change according to how you feel, and move them from your head to a sheet of paper, transforming your ideas into a plan. This method removes unsolicited emotions and makes the plan plain.

Throw away the being-average-survival script, and let's learn the wealth-building script. It is by design that we will go from backwards thinking to forward thinking. EVERYTHING STARTS WITH THE HEAD, so HEADS-UP!

MINDSET CHANGING

I know you are Perry Carson II, but you have to see yourself as Perry "the first", Alan 1st, or Thomas 1st. You will be the first in your family to do a lot of things. Look at it this way: If there is a family tradition of poverty and lack, then backwards thinking was dominant. Then YOU were born. You are different. There's a different beat that you hear and march to. The sheet music to your life hasn't even been written yet. Each step is a note, and the masterpiece has started. You will not enter this world and exit this world with no one knowing your name. 'YOU ARE THE ONE'! The game changer. Yes, but wait, the name changer, too. You are either anointed or annoying. Choose the first.

No more will anyone be born and die as adults, leaving the family where it was when they came or worse off spiritually, mentally, emotionally and definitely not financially. You had an entire lifetime to help them move forward and you didn't. Shame on you for loving yourself so much and never maturing to love others. You must move from immaturity to maturity in all things.

Follow me. You are born as a baby. You are selfish, crying when you are wet and hungry with no thought of anyone else. As a toddler, your friend Benson comes over and your parent hears a smack then runs to your room to discover you hit your friend because he grabbed your toy, and you are whining 'mine.' Your parents are aware they must teach you to share because you were born selfish. You are now older, volunteering and doing mission work, putting others first, mature now. You don't want to die a baby. Wouldn't that be backwards to you? You have an entire lifetime; you've gotta get it right. This is it, friend; you are not getting another life to repeat the same thing. That's backwards. Hey YOU, no more backwards thinking.

You must start with the end in mind. The process of building wealth is a mathematical design; it will not happen by accident. Luke 14:28 (NKJV) says, "For which of you, intending to build a tower, does not sit down first and count the cost to see if he has enough to finish it?"

I spent eight years of my career in television. One of my first assignments was as a photographer. There is a secret to keeping your camera in focus. You should first zoom in tight to the subject farthest away and focus. You can now zoom out wide and everything between the subjects farthest away and the subject closest to you should still be in focus. Focus on your end number. Example: $10,000,000. Decide the time frame needed to achieve this goal. Write down all the details of materials and resources needed for this project down to the lowest common denominator. Finally, winners start now. NO Waiting! Decide!

A few keys:

FEAR DOESN'T STAND A CHANCE WHEN YOU UNDERSTAND.

I believe success is 1 cm on the other side of whatever you said you don't want to do.

You are only one step away from starting. SO TAKE THE STEP. You will be so glad you did.

To succeed you must learn how to be a "COP":

CLEAR
OBSESSED
PURPOSEFUL

Only a fool thinks he can change the fruit by talking to the fruit. You change the fruit when you change the root. It's the seed that you gotta reach. So, there is a difference between changers and complainers.

"Be careful what you think, because your thoughts run your life." Proverbs 4:23 (NCV).

The first wealth

is health.

RALPH WALDO EMERSON

Kristopher Aaron was born and raised in Chicago, Illinois in 1974. He is 6ft 6in tall and weighs 218lbs.

Syracuse University is his Alma Mater.

After ten years of working in the world of high finance investing and insurance (1998-2008) with companies such as AIG, Chase, Zurich, ING, Primerica, and Allianz, he decided to take his talents to the field of natural health.

He went from selling "Life Insurance" to "Life Assurance".

After seeing so many people in his family including his mother die at the hands of chemotherapy, radiation, surgeries, and pharmaceutical meds, and how most of it could have been avoided if people were willing to change their diet and lifestyle, he decided to become a crusader!!

In Jan 2009, he became a high raw vegan and has maintained that lifestyle to this day. He is also an Ultramarathoner. That is someone who run races usually well over a 50-mile distance. He works as a wellness consultant, trainer, and facilitator for extended Water and Juice Fasts.

His motto is: Self-care leads to Self-love! Your Seed is the only Master Your Future will obey

KRISTOPHER AARON
True Health Begins at a Cellular Level

Health is the New Wealth. Being healthy is the first step to living your best life. It is unquestionably the one thing that most people take for granted. Is health just about being able to make it through the day without any symptoms of illness? Or is true health a deep cellular phenomenon whereby each of the trillions of cells that make up your body are truly happy, thriving, and vibrating at the highest frequencies? Where your energy levels are so high and your passion to live rather than just merely exist renews itself with each new day? True cellular health is the rarest and most valuable commodity on this planet. Health is an achievement. It is deliberate and not arbitrary. It's an awakening and a vibrational frequency. Without it, it's impossible to live your best life.

We live in a sick world that's getting sicker every day. But at the same time, we live in an amazing world that's getting better every day. There are extremes on both ends and we can consciously choose what world we want to create and live in. But as we know, anything worth having is worth paying the price for. Change is the one constant that we have to embrace.

We have to be willing to change our beliefs and be open to new information and new ways of living. I always say, "Marry Principles, But Court Your Beliefs," because most of what we believe is rooted in false knowledge.

False knowledge leads to making mistakes. Making mistakes manifests the dark ages. We call it "Plato's Cave."

1. False Knowledge
2. Making Mistakes (sinning)
3. Manifest the dark ages

Plato's Cave is known as the cave of ignorance. Most of humanity is trapped at this level. Remember the word "sin" means to "miss the mark" or "to make a mistake." Most of us make mistakes (sin) unconsciously. And it has to do with us lacking the basic knowledge of how to live. With that premise in mind, until we escape Plato's Cave, everything is a distraction...EVERYTHING!

Escaping Plato's Cave is how we become fully activated and truly healthy at a cellular level. It leads us to understanding the gospel. Many years ago, it was called the Godspell. They changed it to the Gospel. That became known as the Good News. The word "News" is simply an acronym for north, east, west, and south. The Good News of what? Air, Fire, Earth, And Water. A few there be who find it. Who find what? The answer to the alchemy of cellular health and immortality.

As you will see through my writings, many of the things that you believe about health and nutrition are founded on false knowledge and just flat-out lies. Let us examine air, fire (sunshine), earth (plants), and water.

Air pollution is one of the top causes of death. Chemtrails, cooking soot from homes and restaurants, radiation, greenhouse gases, emissions from animal agriculture, fossil fuels, etc.—it seems as if we are under attack from every direction. There are so many booby traps in the world, but with a little health knowledge and the discipline to act on what you learn, you can reap a much different destiny than your bloodline predecessors. Fresh, clean air is sacred. Plants constantly clean the air. The word plant means "wandering seed." That's why it is so important to keep plants in your home and to get out in nature as often as possible. The Areca Palm is the number one plant for filtering air inside your home. Breath is such an important yet overlooked aspect of health. Deep breathing is an art and a consciousness. Most people are shallow breathers. Deep calls unto deep. Problems happen over time, not overnight. It sometimes takes years to recognize our mistakes and for the effects of our bad habits to manifest.

Remember, you can go weeks without food, but most of us would be dead if we stopped breathing for even just five minutes. Deep diaphragmic breaths are critical to building and maintaining a sound physical flesh house.

The next aspect of the gospel is fire, meaning "sunshine." The sun is the father of all living things. The sun doesn't cause cancer. It exposes cancer. It is the ultimate detoxifier. We are created for a life of fun in the sun. Sunshine is critical to health and happiness. In places where sunshine is limited, depression and illness abound. Places like the North Pole, Antarctica, Alaska, etc., aren't exactly hubs for vacations and retreats. The sun feeds our cells with vital nutrients and free energy by which we thrive. You may not have had a choice of where you were born, but you most definitely have a choice as to where you live as an adult. Choose to live in places where sunshine is prominent most of the time. Or at the very least, travel to those places a few times a year to soak up some sun and be revitalized at a deeper level.

The next aspect of the gospel is earth or plants. All information comes from plants. Raw plant foods in the form of fruits and vegetables are the most magical and healing foods. Raw plant food is medicine. Fruits and Vegetables vibrate much higher than any other foods. They are the easiest to assimilate and digest. These are our natural foods to thrive on. They are loaded with life, love, minerals, fiber, water and higher frequencies. The "raw-er" you are, the more synchronicities and magic that you attract to your life. You experience more freedom and abundance when you consume raw fruits and vegetables consistently and in great variety. 99.9% of all food on earth is raw plant food. Fruits, greens, vegetables, nuts, seeds, herbs, mushrooms, sprouts, sea veggies, and superfoods will never go out of style. Eating these foods is a path to beauty and true energy.

All animals on this planet except humans and domesticated pets eat 100% raw. Raw means real. I'm not talking about raw animal products. I'm talking about uncooked and uncultivated fruits and vegetables. We lose enzymes and biophotons when we cook our food. But more on that later in this chapter. Fruits and vegetables help to keep our bodies and bloodstreams in an alkaline state, whereby our pH is at a healthy level between 7.0 for our saliva and 7.4 for our blood. PH is short for "potential of hydrogen." Cooking our food destroys a nutrient that feeds one of our senses. Human beings are a six-sense species, not five sense. We tend to lose or greatly diminish our sixth sense the more that we cook and process our foods. No free animal tampers with its food. Cooking doesn't exist in Nature. Whenever you add fire to anything, it destroys. Fire is a double-edged sword. I know that this is a very tough truth for most people simply because eating cooked food is normal for most of us and the idea of even remotely giving up a smidgen of our pleasures is not gonna happen with most. But once you "taste and see" how amazing real food tastes, especially when your body and palate are clean, then you wouldn't dream of going back to the old life.

The next aspect is water. Water is the elixir of life. Water is a solvent. It is the ultimate purifier. Drinking pure spring water is vital to a healthy body. Water keeps things flowing and easy. Most of our water should come from our food in the form of raw fruits and vegetables but the remainder should come in liquid form. If you are fortunate enough to live near a wild spring to harvest your own spring water, then that's best.

www.findaspring.com is a great resource to use to locate spring water in your area. Otherwise, store-bought water or buying an ionizer are your other options. Choose wisely when you choose drinking water. Many bottled waters are highly acidic. Test the waters yourself or find out the healthiest waters. Water nurtures and sustains all living things. Water is revered as a symbol of humility and service. It seeks nothing for itself and it always flows to the lowest spots. Water feeds the two primary fluids in our body, the blood and the lymph. Our blood is the kitchen. Our lymph is the bathroom. Water has a major impact on the 3 cycles of food:

1. Consumption
2. Absorption
3. Elimination

Water is the ultimate pain reliever. Just flood your body with water and wash your miseries away. Drinking enough water raises vibrational frequency, which leads us to 10 things that lower vibrational frequency:

1. Hard alcohol
2. Junk food
3. Animal foods
4. White sugar
5. Medication
6. Holding onto the past
7. Listening to heavy metal music consistently
8. Yelling and arguing
9. Watching the news consistently
10. Poverty

Let's contrast this with 10 things that raise vibrational frequency:

1. Raw Plant Food
2. Classical Music
3. Yoga
4. Removing mucoid plaque from your colon
5. Eating and juicing raw green leafy vegetables
6. Opulence
7. Cleanliness
8. Burning sage and lavender oil
9. Forgiveness
10. Walking on the beach

True health does not happen by chance. It happens by design. You have to really want it. You have to say no to the booby trap of immediate gratification and embrace the art of delayed gratification. But above all, listen to your intuition. Your intuition is your personal success mechanism. No one can hear it but you, so stop asking others their opinions about how you should live your life. Your intuition is the voice of God, that still, small voice that leads you ever so gently. The sooner that you recognize and listen to this voice, the happier and healthier that you will be. It takes courage to follow your own path. Most people go along to get along. But that doesn't have to be you. Don't follow the herd. The herd is headed toward the abyss and over a cliff. We are living in the New Age of "Aqua-Gnosis," which means knowledge of the liquids. We are being called to purge, purify, and perfect our bodies so that they are fit for a lifetime of love and service to one another.

But be forewarned: There are no shortcuts. You must be willing to learn, unlearn, and re-learn a few things. The way that we used to do things quite frankly won't cut it moving forward. There are two ways to make a mistake:

1. Applying false knowledge
2. Not applying what we already know

The number one reason why people don't apply what they know is fear. Fear is a cruel taskmaster. Most of our fears are subconscious. There are only two frequencies in the universe: Love and fear. We must raise our frequencies to tap into the love vibrations and to free us from the fear vibrations. What we eat greatly influences the frequencies that we tap into. YOU ARE WHAT YOU EAT is written in flaming letters on the fleshly tablets of the human heart. It is an inescapable reality of quantum physics. Cleansing our bodies and changing our diets is the first step to experiencing true health at a cellular level. There simply is no other way. The first step is the most difficult. It is self-renunciation. It's going through the process of cleansing your body through an extended water and juice fast.

Everyone is different, and we all need individual analysis on where we are and where we need to be. But most people of a sound constitution can handle a water fast of 21 days. If you're someone who takes medication or has a health condition, then separate protocols would be necessary. But most people can handle a water fast for 21 days and 21 nights to cleanse and purify the body. If water only is too intimidating for you, well then, I extend the olive branch of adding fresh live juices and herbal teas to the mix. Fasting is the most powerful form of healing and cleansing the body. It takes you to the lowest levels, so that you can be exalted to the highest levels. The word fast means "to make strong". There's no way around it. Your body is unclean. I'm not talking about the outside; I'm talking about the inside. Fasting is the best way to clean out the inside of our bodies. Undergoing an extended fast can be likened to entering into a new dimension. It's exciting and freeing. It's not easy, but it's not hard either. It's something that you just have to do for yourself to really experience the benefits. Because we live in such a food dominant culture, it can be hard giving up your favorite delicacies for even a short amount of time, but when you do, you start to realize how much better you look and feel when you give up food for a period of time. Fasting opens doors. The number 21 represents breakthrough. We call it the "three sevens". Three represents renewal. Seven represents completion. Fasting on water and fresh juices is for everyone.

Fasting is a choice, not a requirement. It's a rabbit hole that leads to a better quality of life with a better quality of people. Fasting cannot be defeated nor beat. It is the most powerful spiritual weapon that we've been given. It trumps all obstacles. It represents the highest level of delayed gratification. Remember, we are under the "Hunger Spell." True hunger does not occur in the stomach. True hunger is a watering of the throat. Most people can go weeks before they experience true hunger. We eat mostly because of emotional reasons. We're bored, we're lonely, we're stressed, etc. Overcoming our food demons is a necessary step in our goal of achieving divine health at a cellular level. Fasting, especially water fasting, facilitates that process better than anything else, which leads me to one of the most profound discoveries of this age. I call it the "5 Mistakes".

I shall start with mistake number 5 and work back up to number 1.

MISTAKE NUMBER 5: ADDING CHEMICALS TO OUR FOOD SUPPLY

The chemical revolution of the 1940s bought about a new phenomenon. We started added pesticides, herbicides, fungicides, preservatives, and a litany of ingredients that are difficult to spell let alone pronounce. This bought about more damage to our health in the name of profits. The way to overcome this is simply always buy organic or heirloom. If you are in a position to grow your own food, then that would be ideal.

MISTAKE NUMBER 4: PROCESSED FOOD

Eating processed food has a detrimental long-term effect on our health and consciousness. Processed food is everywhere. The good news is that there are so many healthy substitutes nowadays that we can choose from. In this age, we've been given a choice. Here are 10 of the most common processed foods found in American Supermarkets and some healthier alternatives.

1. Cheese – Cheese is one of the most common culprits. It's known to cause mucus, constipation, and acidosis. A healthy alternative is raw nut cheese made from soaked cashews. You

can google a ton of recipes online. Or organic soy cheeses from health food stores.

2. Bread – You've never seen a "bread tree" growing wild in nature. Most bread on the market is not suitable for human consumption. It's been "enriched" with white flour, sugar, paste, and many other ingredients that you would need a dictionary to define. Either make your own sprouted, organic bread or choose the healthier "Ezekiel Bread" from health food stores or Whole Foods.

3. Crackers – A healthy alternative would be to purchase a dehydrator and make your own flax crackers or kale chips.

4. Pasta – Pasta is one of the heaviest foods that one can eat. It's filled with "enriched" flour and other acid-causing ingredients. A far healthier option is to simply spiralize some Zucchini or Squash and make your own pasta. It tastes so much better and is far healthier.

5. Rice – Rice is a common starch that many people enjoy. Quinoa is a healthier alternative that taste amazing. Black Wild Rice is perhaps the healthiest variety of rice.

6. Cereals – Those morning breakfast cereals are so loaded with empty calories. Choose the healthier varieties from health food stores and use the nut milks instead of cow milk, which is highly acidic and mucus forming.

7. Potato Chips – Kale Chips are a much healthier option. But if you must eat potato chips then ALWAYS choose organic.

8. French Fries – One of the top "comfort foods" for many people. Avoid if possible but choose organic if you must indulge.

9. Pastries – If you have a sweet tooth. I recommend eating fruit. Muffins, bagels, donuts, scones, cookies, etc. do not exist in nature. If you must indulge, then choose the plant-based variety with raw coconut sugar or other natural sweeteners.

10. Salad Dressing – Most salad dressings on the market are so unhealthy, loaded with sugars, salts, and oils. It's best to just make your own. There are a ton of recipes online nowadays. A high-speed blender is all that you would need to make most of the recipes.

MISTAKE NUMBER 3: EATING PLANTS that
we are not bio – adapted to eat. A good example of this would be certain grains and grasses.

MISTAKE NUMBER 2: EATING ANIMALS

We are not designed by nature to eat and digest any animal. We are not carnivores by design. We don't have claws and fangs to rip into flesh. Isn't it easier to sneak up on lettuce than it is a rabbit? Meat has no fiber and is very acidic. Animal agriculture is one of the most destructive things to the environment and to our physical health. The good news is that we are no longer in the dark ages. There are so many healthier plant-based and raw vegan options for almost every food. Choose to live cruelty free. Choose life. Study other ways to satisfy your dietary needs. Meat is a secondhand protein. Eat those things that want you to eat them, like fruit and veggies. Stop eating things that run from you. That's a golden clue from the universe that maybe you shouldn't be eating it.

MISTAKE NUMBER 1: COOKED FOOD. ALSO KNOWN AS THE "FALL OF MANKIND."

Cooking our food destroys the enzymes and life force found in the food. It destroys a nutrient that feeds one of our senses. We are a six-sense species, not five sense. Cooking destroys the biophotons with the food. A biophoton is coherent sunlight energy that all living systems store in the center of their cells. And the cells use that energy to communicate. Eating cooked food disconnects us from our natural selves and unleashes our dark side. If you need proof of that then simply look at the state of the world or closely examine your own behavior. Test yourself for 91 days. Stop eating cooked food. Eat only live fruits, vegetables, nuts, seeds, salads, smoothies, juices, etc. and see how amazing you look and feel.

Going on an extended fast on water and fresh juices will correct all five mistakes on a temporary basis. We call it a "solid food vacation."

Fasting is truly what your body wants the most. It's how we take back control of the one thing that is controlling us: GLUTTONY.

Remember, almost everyone is under the Hunger Spell, whether they know it or not. Food is the universal kryptonite of most human beings. The quickest and surest way to conquer the hunger spell is to go on a solid food vacation for a minimum of 21 days. But 42 days would probably be more ideal and effective. I know people who have fasted 100 days on nothing but water and fresh live juices, and the results are always amazing and eye opening.

You may think that sounds extreme. But not to me. Extreme to me is living the rest of my life on dialysis. Or wearing adult diapers. Or open-heart surgery and all of the other invasive and painful things that hospitals put their patients through. It's not worth it. An ounce of prevention is worth a ton of cure. Don't let it happen in the first place. Your life and body are worth it. The human body isn't to be toyed or tinkered with. It does not accept replacement parts unless it's drugged into submission.

In America, the top five causes of death are: heart disease, cancer, iatrogenic illness (doctor-induced), diabetes, and lower respiratory illness. What we eat is what's killing us. And unless we make some radical changes, then things are only going to get worse.

The bottom line is this: You have to change your diet. You can't eat the way that you grew up eating. The good news is that there are more healthy options and information available today than ever before. But you must choose to make the upgrade.

Raised in Terrell Texas **Tony Stephens** is a National Sales Director and agency owner with an international financial services organization. He currently has 13 offices that are spread across the great state of Texas. Tony's passion was always to help and serve others and he and his wife Paula found a way to do so 30 years ago in the financial services industry. His individual agency has placed more than 4 billion in life insurance coverage over his 30-year career. Tony is a member of the African American Leadership Council, Financial Independence Council and was recognized as MVP. Tony serves as a mentor for several men and women who desire to be entrepreneurs.

He also enjoys motivational speaking and was blessed to be a featured speaker at the Georgia Dome with an audience of more than 55,000 in attendance.

Tony has been married to Paula Stephens for more than 31 years and they have 2 sons, Tony II and Christopher. He also has 1 granddaughter Chandler.

TONY STEPHENS
Mental Hygiene

A few months ago, I took my nephews to Disney World. We flew from Dallas, so you know the drill: two boys with their uncle in the car, then an airport, then a plane, then the hotel check-in, and settling in for the night. For them it was all pure fun. It was fun for me too but, being the resident authority figure dealing with two high-octane kids, I had a different job.

It was their first time on an airplane. Their pure joy of being high in the air was more than just a pleasure to watch. It was contagious. It was an atmosphere. I felt an excitement being there with them I hadn't felt in years. As they exited their first flight, I saw the joy in their eyes. It was an inarticulate joy. Wow! The feeling of being free from the limits of our physical ability—flying, unshackled from the restrictions of land travel. It was a feeling of liberation and empowerment, a feeling I was already familiar with.

This same feeling came to me when I made the transition from employee to entrepreneur. It felt like I had witnessed the invention of fire. I had escaped the self-imposed limits of my individual abilities. The limits were not only broken from my income, they were broken from my personal efforts. Now I had a team, a business! Wow! This shared feeling stayed with me all the way through hotel check-in, dinner, and the evening's bedtime rituals. It was a moment of true reflection.

Morning rolled around and the boys were bouncing off the walls. From the first second they woke up they were ready for anything—anything except what I said to them.

"Bath time," I told them. "Who's first: Kevin or Jay?"

"We just took a bath yesterday!" Kevin said.

"Ok, I understand that but it's a new day, all right? Who's gonna take a bath first?"

After I finally got them bathed, we went to Disney World and had a great morning standing in lines, riding the rides, and heckling Goofy and Mickey. Being with them at Disney World was like being with them on the plane. Their pure excitement and their unalloyed optimism for the gifts the day would bring became mine.

As a young adult I lived in poverty. Living in America—in what is arguably the greatest country on earth, in the greatest hour in the history of mankind—I felt as if I were living next door to Disney World and was not able to afford a ticket to enter the park. I could look into the park, see the advertisements, and watch other families enjoying a life I wasn't privileged or able to experience. All of it was in my view but out of my reach. Disney is a place where a child's imagination is challenged with the questions *Why not? Is it really possible?* Being blessed with God's greatest gift to humankind, a full imagination, I felt there was no known place in this universe outside of Earth that you can make your dreams come true. Everything the world promised must be possible to achieve.

Taking your child to Disney World is like our Heavenly Father placing us on earth to dream and ask ourselves *why not?* To ask *is it possible?* To ask *why not live your dream?* Nothing is impossible with optimism. There is no such thing as a pessimistic developer. You should always ask *why not?* God does not torture his children. Whatever you see, you can be. Your dreams are a picture of your finished future.

As I watched my nephews' joy at Disney World, immersing myself in their energy, I thought, *if you hold a caterpillar in your hand, then ask, 'Where is the butterfly?' Its future is inside of it. If you hold an acorn in your hand, then ask, 'Where is the oak tree?' Its future is inside of it. Your dreams, your imagination is fighting to live in material form. Where is your future? It's inside of you.*

After we ate lunch—a corndog at Magic Kingdom—they were wilting a little, so we went back to the room for a rest.

When we walked in the door I said, "Who's gonna take a bath first, Kevin or Jay?"

"We took a bath this morning!" Jay protested.

"That's fine, but we can't ignore the fact that y'all stink. So who's gonna bathe first, cause you're not going around with me smelling like you've been wrestling all morning. So no, you have to take a bath!"

When we were cleaned up and rested, we went to the park again. As soon as we hit the ground back at Disney World, the boys immediately picked up where they left off—right back in their joy, as if they had never been tired, as if they had never been dirty. I thought about how easy it is for dreams to disappear, for optimism to vanish, even though their promise is always there waiting for us.

The most copious, abundant place of goals and dreams is in the cemetery. People take their dreams to the grave. Their dreams die inside of them because dreams are time sensitive. An acorn is a seed that can be placed on a shelf for five, ten, fifteen, or even twenty years, never experiencing its true purpose or potential. Like the sitting acorn, many of us remain on the shelf in fear and doubt for five, ten, fifteen, or even twenty years, leaving our dreams lying dormant inside of us.

What God has for the acorn is for the acorn, and what God has for you is for you. However, for the acorn to open its future and potential to grow into an oak tree it has to accept the responsibility of being planted. And we have the responsibility to manifest our dreams. Our dreams may be God-given, but the manifestation requires our personal effort.

After posing all morning for pictures with my nephews at Disney World, I began to think about the family portrait in my living room. If I were to cut that finished portrait into a hundred pieces and place those jagged parts in a box, I would have a puzzle. To effectively reassemble the pieces, I'd need a vivid image of the whole picture in the forefront of my mind. That's why we need the picture on a jigsaw puzzle's box top: so that we can imagine what we are trying to recreate.

But the idea of the final puzzle isn't enough. Physical action is required to reassemble the finished picture. If someone gives you a huge jigsaw puzzle as a gift, you might open it, see all the identical-looking pieces jumbled up inside, decide the job is too difficult, and stick the box on the back shelf of a closet, never to be completed. In that case, the picture on the box top is useless; it takes willpower, time, and work to sort the pieces out, determine how they fit together, and assemble the puzzle. Sometimes people put their own lives, their greatest dreams, on the back shelf of a closet and never complete the ideal version of their own futures. The puzzle of your life is there inside you, in pieces waiting to be connected. We only put those pieces together when we are positive, we can do it.

Bible prophecy is accurate because it is the finished history of mankind in God's mind. This is why it comes together so seamlessly. This is hard for us to grasp because humanity is trapped in time while God lives outside of time.

Our afternoon at Disney World seemed timeless as the boys and I made our way through the complicated landscape of attractions. As we wandered, I found myself picturing a maze. If you are walking in a complicated, dark maze you can lose hope as you attempt to find your way through, feeling there is no way out. But if you are able to stand above the maze it becomes obvious how all the pathways fit and connect to get from the entry to the exit. In the same way, if you're able to be above the park (in a helicopter, for example) and see it from a different vantage point, the once-imposing landscape will appear much smaller, and the borders of the park will become visible.

Man is created in God's image, but he lives and is completely trapped in the maze of time. God lives above time, completely outside of time. He is not trapped in time. This allows God to see the full picture. He sees the entrance and the exit. He sees the beginning of your life and the end of your life, as if He were looking at a finished puzzle.

This is where faith comes in. You must believe in your vision. Your dreams are informed by your environment. Believe with your work ethic. Your dreams are simply a part of your unlived reality and future.

Those dreams you think are impossible and have ignored are a picture of your finished future. There are no pessimistic developers. There isn't enough space for your dream and pessimism to co-exist. You must exercise faith and positive thinking. You must learn to create an environment of intentional optimism. A negative mind cannot, and will not, give birth to a beautiful dream life.

Finally, our day at Disney World came to an end. All of us were tired. All of us were sweaty and wilted. When we got back to the room I asked, "Who gets the first bath?"

"Again!?" they squealed together, like a couple of cartoon characters.

I said, "Look guys, this room is too small for me to be smelling you all night. Who's bathing first!?"

On this trip, my nephews were focused on having as much fun as possible every second of the day. And my job, as the mentor in the situation, was to help them achieve their goals while fulfilling their overall trip strategy. This included safety and good hygiene because without taking care of those matters, we'd all have less fun. It was hard for them to see that, and hard for them to grasp that good physical hygiene was directly related to the pleasure they'd take in our trip. In the same way, it's hard for many of us to see how good mental hygiene is the foundation of our ability to make our dreams become our reality.

On this trip, Disney World became more than an amusement park to me; it was place of self-discovery.

"Tony," I told myself, "you have stinking thinking! You are mentally musty!" As I stood in awe of the full flowering of my nephews' optimistic imaginations, all I could do was doubt my real potential. Disney World became my mental gymnasium. I was being challenged to dream again. I was in full contact with the unlimited possibilities of human imagination. Was I dreaming too small? Am I mentally musty? I never knew how negative I was until I was confronted with the question *why not?*

I had been teaching my nephews the importance of physical hygiene. But it became overwhelmingly obvious as we walked through Disney, seeing the full manifestations of the possibilities of humanity, that we are more than this meat suit, our physical body. Physically, we can enjoy our dream life but in order to fully realize it, we must imagine and create it mentally. I was telling them about managing their physical hygiene but was neglecting my own mental hygiene.

Suppose you are at a gym with four friends after a hard, hot workout. Everyone stinks to an equal degree. Everyone gets into the car to leave, and it's okay because you all are immersed in a common smell. It's awful; however, you all are immersed in it. You then leave to shower; now you are refreshed. If you get back in the car with the others, it becomes very obvious that now your friends all stink, and it's almost intolerable.

As a child I was full of optimistic possibility. Most of us believe as kids we can be and do anything. Without bills to pay our only responsibility is to dream. You imagine being president, or a doctor, or a lawyer living in the best neighborhood, driving the best car. You can live this dream called America.

Once you leave home and your parents' protection, you discover quickly the reality of how limiting a fast-food worker's income can be. You find yourself driving the worst cars and not being able to afford a decent life. Maybe then you stop dreaming. Ten or twenty years pass like twenty minutes! With an active diet of negativity, you forget how to dream. All of the ideas in your head are negative, pessimistic. You now have the disease of "stinking thinking." It's not obvious because you are immersed in it. All of the people around you have the same smelly, stinking thinking. It is not until you step away and get an optimistic mental shower that you are exposed to and confronted with what is possible if you only dream.

As with my nephews, as with the gym workout with friends, physical hygiene is mandatory. But what we need most is good mental hygiene. You can't dream or live to the level of your imagination with negative self-talk. My ideas smelled of negative self-talk.

I knew how my nephews were feeling; they both smelled the same so why bathe? This was another "aha" moment! It's true what my father once told me: "A man is known by the successive choirs of his peers." Now it was obvious I needed to change my peers. In a moment of reflection, I remembered feeling that once I was exposed to an environment of optimism, my immediate response was to tell my family and friends about my dreams and my potential. I had just experienced my first mental shower of optimism. I felt fresh, alive, and free from the grips of negativity and doubt. I was excited but my joy wasn't shared. My friends had stinking thinking, and a stench that they were not aware of because they all smelled the same. I had a mental shower, but they hadn't. They were totally unaware of the negativity they had lived with for years.

I had left the room, cleansed myself, and returned to the stench, the awful smells that I had become accustomed to. My nephews were physically musty, but my peers were mentally musty and had no desire to take a mental shower. They had no desire to confront their negativity or their pessimistic attitudes. I had changed and there was no returning for me. I won't accept poor mental hygiene anymore. I decided to embrace the same discipline to manage my mental hygiene that I apply to my physical hygiene.

To achieve intentional mental hygiene, you must bathe your mind in optimism through mental immersion. You can do this by reading books on self-development, connecting with positive peers daily, and listening to successful mentors daily. You must hold a passionate belief, and you must have an optimistic vision of your best life, keeping these ideas clear in your imagination and with an active commitment to a full physical expression of these ideas. Do it now! Build it as you imagine it! This is how you build this dream called America.

• • • • • •

"How was your trip?" their grandmother said, hugging them when I got my nephews home.

"We had a great time! But Uncle Tony made us take three baths in one day!"

We all can identify with that reaction. We were all kids once, and someone had to wrestle us to bathe. On the trip, the boys were focused on one thing: having as much fun as possible. That was their goal. They weren't thinking about the whole trip – all the time spent together in the car and in the hotel room; three human bodies in close proximity for hours on end. And they weren't thinking of the three of us as a team, working together, not only to enjoy riding the rides and tugging on Mickey's arm, but also to get there and back again as safely and comfortably as possible. They needed me to see to their well-being, but I needed them to remind me to take care of my own mental hygiene.

Flying to Disney World, traveling by air for the first time, my nephews were filled with an infectious optimism that, if it could be bottled and passed around, would save the world. Maintaining that joy, that pure positivity is, I think, impossible to do alone. It takes an immersion and re-immersion; it takes building a team and being a player on that team. It takes optimism's spa treatment. Rinse and repeat!

OUR LEGACY

PERSEVERANCE, RESILIENCY, AND MOTIVATION

Observing my parents while being in this environment enabled me to realize that there are two choices: You can either be active in control of your own narrative or you can stay passive and simply watch someone else do it for you. It makes you look at that so-called 'glass ceiling' and reveals that it's actually just a transparent stage that is merely a stepping stone for your next big move. Utilizing this mindset took me from proudly serving in the military to pursuing higher education in the United Kingdom.

Through faith and this mindset, I've been able to accomplish many of the things I fought and prayed for. In the span of eight years I've worked with some of the most elite men and women in the armed forces, started a career in broadcasting, and have been blessed with the opportunity to create further opportunities and platforms for myself and others. It is paramount that perseverance, resiliency, and motivation become your ethos so that you can overcome the fears of the hypothetical 'maybes' or 'what ifs.' I can confidently say that one's goals are achievable, but one must recognize that true wealth really does start in the mind, that sacrifice and pain are just building blocks and that you are truly the deciding factor of your own success.

Mattison Lee Williams, 27, son of Lee & Margo Williams.

• • • • • •

NO LIMITS

This mindset has freed me in terms of my vision. I am able to dream and set goals for the future that I wouldn't have been able to see and believe that I could achieve if I hadn't been taught the values and principles of financial freedom. I know that there is a way out of the nine-to-five so that I can provide generational wealth for my family and their families. I can help others reach their goals and dreams as well! I am a vessel to freedom, and I know that there are no limits placed on my life and success! I thank God for my parents taking the steps necessary to provide a better future and life for us.

Morgan Williams, 21, daughter of Lee & Margo Williams

• • • • • •

THE PERFECT EXAMPLE

Growing up, Mom always demonstrated the importance of perseverance, hard work, and self-improvement. She was always the first one up and moving in our family, even on vacation, preparing for the start of a new day and a new opportunity. My mom emphasized the benefit of consistently working on yourself through self-reflection, assessment, and adaptation. Her leadership skills in life and business, including how she speaks to others, how she speaks to herself, and how she fosters growth from the bottom up, provided me with the perfect example of how to lead and accomplish the goals on which I set my sights. The late nights and early mornings have inspired me to push forward through each road-block, setback, growing pain, and success that I have encountered.

Kristen Turner, 30, daughter of Rene & Mel Turner

• • • • • •

BALANCE

When I think about my mom, I think of balance. She's a woman of faith and a business woman. She cares for others, and she also knows the value of self-care. I have learned from her that I don't have to be just one thing. I don't have to let society, or my mistakes, or my insecurities determine my future. She taught me that I can choose my path if I am focused and intentional. I have vivid memories of coming into my parents' bathroom in the mornings and watching my mom read her daily affirmations and study Bible verses as she got ready for work. Her car was full of motivational tapes, then eventually CDs and now podcasts. She spoke and continues to speak positively about herself and her business, always saying "I get to" instead of "I have to" and "I will" instead of "I can't." Her success has been no accident. It's the result of years of diligence, positivity, and planning. She is my biggest cheerleader and my greatest role model. She inspires me every day, and I credit all of my success to my parents' unconditional support.

Courtney Turner, 24, daughter of Rene & Mel Turner

• • • • • •

I WAS SET UP

At an early age it was planted in me from my parents that I was special. I knew that I was supposed to succeed because all of my life I've been around success and it let me know that's what I was supposed to be and be doing.

My mom would remind me daily: "Keondra, you're a beautiful, smart chocolate princess", is what she would always say. I now understand she was planting seeds of self-assurance, self-esteem and self-love that would grow.

Because I heard this so frequently, I grew up believing what I heard.

My mom recalls when I was four years old my pre-k teacher, Mrs. Walker, called her one afternoon and told her one of the students called me an ugly name. The teacher was so impressed when she heard my reply.

She says I told the student, "NO, I'm a beautiful chocolate princess." The teacher told my mom, "You should be so proud. I had to call and share this with you."

At six years of age I started playing sports, all sports, but I did exceptionally well at softball and basketball. My dad coached some of my teams and assisted on nearly all of my teams in some fashion.

I can remember when I changed, and it was not enough to just be on a team; I wanted to be a starter on the team, then I wanted to always be on a winning team.

I realized because of my upbringing I had an expectation to win in whatever I did. I hated losing. By the time I got to high school I had been playing basketball for years and had traveled all over the country playing on various AAU and travel teams.

I was ready, and I earned a scholarship to have my college education paid for. Those were some of the happiest days of my life. I wasn't just getting ready for high school prom and graduation, but I was also celebrated at my high school in Houston, Texas in the auditorium with a huge signing party in front of all of my peers. I received a full athletic scholarship.

I graduated college with a degree in early childhood development and joined our family business shortly after graduation.

Today I'm 29 years of age and a Regional Vice President in our family business. Within the past six months God blessed me to close on my first home.

The choices my parents made set me up for success and it has been passed down to a third generation, my daughter, Kennedy Gabrielle Osagie.

The choices you make set you up for failure or for success. My parents set me up for success. I have seen what winning looks like all of my life, and as a result of that I knew I was supposed to be achieving, whatever the endeavor.

My mom has been most influential because she taught me at an early age how to set goals, plan, and how to think things through.

Some common phrases that were embedded in me and my brother Kenneth were to never give up. Work hard and do your best. Respect the process and you will get the result; she would always say.

Because of the investment and all the positive deposits my parents made in me and my brother, I knew what to do with my daughter Kennedy.

Kennedy is such a special gift. God has great things in store for her. She attends a state-of-the-art academy that is preparing her and challenging her intellectually. She is eight years of age and flourishing with a 4.0 GPA. Kennedy has performed in plays and led her school assembly with her first solo.

Kennedy loves achieving and she is often referred to as such a caring child. She's always optimistic, with a very competitive spirit. She is always determined to do her best. She was just celebrated as the parish champion in Jefferson Parish for the second year in row for short put.

It's no wonder she's a champion, and she has been reciting these affirmations since she was four years old.

YOU WILL HAVE WHAT YOU SAY

I'm a champion
I'm a winner
I'm smart
I'm beautiful
I'm a child of God

Kennedy Gabrielle Osagie, 8, daughter or Keondra Prevost
Keondra Prevost, 29, daughter of Joyclen Prevost

• • • • • •

I'M LIVING WHAT I LEARNED

I would say I am a beneficiary of a strong legacy of love, commitment and dedication.

The legacy of love and strong foundation of commitment and dedication in every endeavor that my parents have paved will live on in us for many generations to come.

While growing up I saw daily discipline and sacrifice in both of my parents. My parents had strong dedication to our family and an unwavering faith to do something special.

My sister and I came first in whatever they did. My mother worked for a number of hospitals until she could find the right one that would accommodate our family dynamic, allowing her the flexibility to cater to our schedules. There were times that my father would do doubles to carry the load for additional expenses for special camps, tutors, multiple band instruments, or whatever the need or want. They were doing it for us and our family.

Nothing is going to be handed to you. You are blessed with the privilege to do something great with your life. Entitlement is a crutch.

I value work ethic because it's what I saw.

WHAT I SAW: Strong work ethic in my parents.

WHAT I APPLIED: I will admit I was the student who went to college and did not know what I wanted to do. I did not initially have the success I could have had if I had applied myself fully and enrolled with the intention of excelling. I grew up in an environment of stability, with loving, engaging and very involved parents. We had comforts and luxuries some of my friends could only dream about.

College was a good experience and I graduated with a BS in Business Administration.

About 90 days after graduation an opportunity was presented for me to go back to school in an Aptech Express Program, but this time, and for the first time, I chose to fully commit to this program and be dedicated to learning as much as I could. I fully committed 100 percent and finished with a second degree in Allied Science in just one year. Upon completion I was blessed with several offers. The discipline and hard work have paid off tremendously. Within my first two years I have achieved several certifications that have opened up other doors and further advanced my career.

After applying what was instilled in me from the examples I saw in my parents, I have excelled in my career path in just a few years. Becoming a one percenter, I have stabilized my finances and advanced in my career.

Finding something you love to do and having the discipline to stick to it is what I learned from my parents and it has been a compass for me in my life.

What a way to honor my parents' legacy of loving people, having a good work ethic, and being dedicated and committed to your life's purpose.

Kenneth Prevost Jr., 30, son of Joyclen Prevost

• • • • • •

GROWING UP WITH AN ENTREPRENEUR

I grew up in inner-city Baltimore. I went to public schools for most of my school years, where I was told to focus on getting good grades and a good job. If you're lucky, on my side of town, that's a good government job. Although I looked like a regular girl, I was so different. In high school I was known as the "rich girl," but ironically it was not because I wore fancy or designer clothes because I did not. I was called the rich girl because my mom was able to drop me off and pick me up every day. I was called the rich girl because we took amazing trips frequently. I was called a rich girl because my mother exposed me to a lifestyle and as a result, my mindset was very different than many of the people growing up in inner-city Baltimore. I didn't fit in with the in-crowd.

Limiting beliefs are real and unfortunately can be placed on other people. My mom taught me that you can be anything that you want to be; just make sure you own it. It was obvious that others had not been taught this principle, including the adults around me. When I was in high school some of the teachers would tell us students that we could only be as good as our environment. They would place their limiting beliefs upon us and tell us things like our college experience would be limited by what our family could afford. Thankfully, I had a mom who told me differently. I had a mom who exposed me to other environments. It still baffles me that there are people who live in East Baltimore who have never been to West Baltimore. If you never take a person (especially a child) out of their environment, they will never see past it. My mother took me out of that environment and put me in an environment with people who were going for more in life. I am not a product of the environment I grew up in but of the environment I was placed in. I believe as parents we have to place our children in environments that will build them up and make them believe in themselves. We must put them in environments that will challenge them to get better. That environment must promote positivity and instill good affirmations in them. This must start at home because unfortunately, it does not always happen at school.

I was also taught that you have to see it before you can seize it. My mom stretched my vision daily. We created vision boards. She asked me about the places I wanted to visit and about the things I wanted to have. We would design my room and the house I wanted to live in. We did vision trips to the nice areas and looked at the homes and I would say, "One day this is the type of community we will live in." We visited nice hotels and made plans to stay there. We then discussed and devised a plan to make these visions become a reality. My mom followed that plan until one day we started going on trips and staying at those nice hotels. Eventually, we started checking things off our goals and dreams list. I learned to always have a plan for my vision because a vision without a plan is just a dream. That was so instrumental in my development. In the area in which I was being raised, people had eyesight, but poor vision. My mom taught me how to mentally remove myself from my physical surroundings and how to mentally create the lifestyle I wanted so that it could manifest.

I also learned from my mom the value of investing at an early age. You must live for today but plan for tomorrow. You have to learn to pay yourself. At an early age I was taught the 10/10/80 rule: 10% God 10% myself and 80% everything else. So often in my community people spent everything they had on material possessions. I learned from my mother that it is not about how much you make, but how much you save and keep. I remember when my mom was featured on the cover of Success Magazine and I, being the proud daughter I am, took the book to show my teacher and friends. In the book it stated her income. The kids were like, "If my mom made that much money, I would have the latest everything!" I told them I wasn't into all of that material stuff, but I had a great portfolio. Learning to invest properly is one way to pass on generational wealth. It's a mindset.

My mother also taught me the power of having an owner's mentality. Proverbs 13:22 says: A good man leaves an inheritance to his children's children. She taught me the importance of passing on generational wealth. We hear about people like the Hiltons who, because of one man, changed their family tree forever. One thing my mom always says is, "I took the no's while you were young so that you don't have to take them now that you are older." She taught me that you can only pass on something you own to your children.

One of the most important things I was taught was to always work on the mind. A good leader is always teaching but a great leader is always learning. As a leader you must always work on your mindset. My mom was always reading or listening to something to help her improve her way of thinking. She always hung around people who spoke positive things. She always made sure I was doing the same. We would read together and listen to things when in the car that were building our minds. Your mindset is the key to success in life. What you think will manifest. If you are always thinking negatively nothing great will ever happen. But if you are always thinking positively and believe in yourself you can go far in life.

My life has been nothing short of amazing because I had an entrepreneur for a mom. I had a great example of what a strong person, not just a woman, but what a strong person is. She showed me that it's not always going to be easy but if you never quit and focus on the prize, not the price, it will be worth the sacrifice. I have done things that most would fear doing. By the time I was 25, I had lived in four different states and became a certified chef. I have followed my dreams, not fearing failure. She showed me that with God and a strong work ethic anything is possible.

I am now an adult and a new mom. I work with my mom in our family business. I go into my future excited that wherever God takes me I have the mindset and skills to conquer it all. I know that my daughter will be successful in life because I will teach her all the things my mom taught me. I will make sure that she will be in the right environment around the right people that will build her up instead of tearing her down. She will follow her dreams and I will be there to support her, just like my mom was there for me. I thank my mom for giving me a life that many are not fortunate to experience. I thank her for being the example I want to follow. I only hope that I am that same type of example for my beautiful daughter, Skylar.

Shanina L. Jones, 30, daughter of Lisa M. Jones

• • • • • •

AN ATTITUDE OF PERSEVERANCE

Growing up in New Orleans I was around a melting pot of different cultures and lifestyles. I was able to see many different ways of life, from people who had the nice houses and cars and what I thought was a luxury lifestyle all the way to the people who lived paycheck to no check. I grew up with kids that wanted to be rappers, ballplayers, doctors, cops, and had friends in many different categories of life, and for that viewpoint I am very grateful because it allowed me to see what the right choices and wrong choices in life could look like. The one thing that many of the different people that I knew growing up had in common was that their parents all worked for someone else. Day in and day out their parents had to go in the rat race of life and take orders from someone else. The one thing that was different in my life compared to the people I knew was that my father had his own business and I understood at a very early age that my life was different from the people that I knew. I was able to see my father get up every day and work for himself and build a business for our family. I didn't realize when I was a young kid, but watching him would shape me into the career path that I have chosen today and that was to join the business with him and to step into a role of learning the financial services business.

One of the main principles that I have learned in business, not only from my father but from other mentors that are in our business, is the importance of having an attitude of perseverance. For me what that means is when things get hard and there seems to be no light at the end of the tunnel, keep pushing forward because nothing in life will become better if you sit and soak in sorrow versus moving down the road to your goals, dreams and desires. I learned that in business your success can boil down to, how mentally tough you could be on a daily basis, and pushing toward the things you want to achieve. Being successful in business or life, period, is a process, and every person's process is different; his or her price tag for what they want may not be the same.

There are many lessons that can be learned in the process of being in business for yourself. For people that I know that tell me that they want to have their own business and want to transition into entrepreneurship, I applaud their bravery because it takes a special individual to go against the grain of being an employee. I let them know that in order to have a high level of success they will have to change who they are as a person and that the same mindset that got them where they are today will not be the same mindset that will take them to the next level.

Luckily for me I was raised in an environment that promoted self-growth through continued learning from the books and audios of people who have been successful in life and taking those principles and applying them to my daily life. Being in business hasn't always been the easiest, hasn't always been the prettiest, but it has been the most self-rewarding thing I have achieved in my life.

Joshua Thomas, 28, son of Sedrick and Tanya Thomas

• • • • • •

LIFE LESSONS FROM MY LOVING FATHER

For a very long time I never really knew what my father's career was. I had a basic understanding, but could never fully comprehend it. When I was a young girl and my dad used to pick me up from school, in his fancy suits, the other kids would always ask me, "What does your dad do?" I would answer with some uncertainty, "Oh he's a business owner". As I got older that same question would always come up and my answer would always change. For a while I told people he was a motivational speaker, then I changed it to a business man, and when I hit my teenage years, I just told everyone he sold life insurance. It wasn't until I was about 15 that I realized he was all of those job titles and much more. He's an entrepreneur, a leader, a coach, a business owner, a financial advisor, and the list goes on. You see, I had been around my father's business all my life but I never paid attention until I was older. I always took notice of all the extravagant trips my dad would take our family on but I would zone out when it was time for his weekly conference calls discussing business.

As I matured, I started to observe his mindset and expertise. Although at the time I didn't know it, as I got older his ideologies were starting to rub off on me. One of the main things I learned from my father was to compartmentalize, separate my business ambitions from the rest of my life and not to allow setbacks to destroy me emotionally and carry over into my personal life. Learning how to develop resiliency is an important lesson I learned from my father's long-term success. Resilient people don't dwell on failures, but acknowledge the situation, learn from the mistakes and move forward.

How we grow up and what we are exposed to during our formative years can play a significant role in who we become. Which is why I consider myself lucky enough to have grown up with a father who is an entrepreneur. Because my father is an entrepreneur, the tone of our conversations is naturally different compared to other parents. He's constantly talking to me about what books I should be reading, what shows I should be watching less of, and always reminding me, I can have anything out of life if I put my mind to it. He has taught me not just to win in one area but win in all areas of life, whether it is wealth, health, or family. As a result of my father creating his own business, I naturally feel drawn to entrepreneurship. With entrepreneurship there's more freedom, more income potential, and it enables me to build the life I want for myself.

My father definitely passed down his entrepreneurial mindset to me which has given me many advantages in life. I now know, you can't wait for opportunities to come to you; you have to grab them. Looking back, that upbringing didn't just help me navigate the professional world, it also proved enormously useful to me as an entrepreneur and as a woman.

Jade Thomas, 24, daughter of Sedrick and Tanya Thomas

• • • • • •

FOR GENERATIONS TO COME

I love this business simply because it provided us with a one in a million kind of lifestyle while helping others at the same time. I will forever be grateful to my parents for making the sacrifice to raise us differently. This business has blessed me with many trips and friendships that will last forever. Because my parents chose to break the generational curse of being broke in our family, we as children have been blessed to grow up to be whatever we want to be because they paid the price for us. I will always remember, "help people save money, make money and eliminate debt"—words to live by. It is wonderful to be able to experience and witness the hard work and dedication of my parents' business. More importantly, our family is in position to keep and grow a successful business or sell it for 10 times its worth. As we continue to mature, grow and develop our business to new heights, we will continue to set the example for other families' financial futures to keep it for generations to come, to continue generational wealth.

Janea, 23 and Maui Evans, 29, daughters of Mike and Regina Evans

· · · · · ·

I BELIEVE

I am who God says I am, and you can be what you want to be, all you have to do is just believe. I believe I am a multimillionaire. I believe I am great. I believe I am beautiful. I believe I can do and be anything.

Mikayla Green, 9 years old, Daughter of Dr. Tasheka L. Green

· · · · · ·

LESSONS FROM HOME

Being in business has the power to transform lives.

My parents both being entrepreneurs has allowed me to have many opportunities throughout my life. I have been able to travel and have a rich and fulfilling life. They've both taught me many life lessons. The most important lesson that I have ever learned from them is that being in the business allows a person to have financial freedom. Being financially free means to have more than enough money without having to work. In business, you have the opportunity to acquire passive income and become financially free. I've also learned that only a few people (less than 1%) are truly financially free. My parents have helped me understand business and inspired me to pursue and dedicate my life to studying business in order to grow as a person and also grow my wealth.

Business starts in the mind. If you want to change your life, change the way you think, and learn to change the way you work. In real life, words do become flesh, so if you want to change your life, change your words. Your mind is the key to making you rich and successful in business.

Taylor Knighton, 17, daughter of Terrill Knighton

• • • • • •

FINANCIAL INTELLIGENCE

Growing up in an environment where both my parents were financially intelligent has given me an advantage in life. Growing up learning how to be financially intelligent gave me an edge that most kids did not have. They taught me many things about being financially intelligent so that I could be prepared for the real world outside of home. In my home my parents taught me different ways to be financially independent. I learned that by starting to invest in the stock market and buying shares you can then sell the shares that you invested in and make money. The money that you could make from the stock market can be used to start buying and investing in rental property or starting your own business. My parents own their own business and are both financially independent. I learned that I could become rich by starting a business or investing, so that one day my passive income, meaning money that I don't work for, could cover my total expenses. I could also retire early and live out my dream. Being taught to be financially intelligent has given me an edge so that it will be much easier to navigate through the world and become financially independent.

Justin Knighton, 15, son of Terrill Knighton

AFTERWORD

It is with great honor that I was able to work with these amazing business women and men. They are some of the most sought-after speakers worldwide and many lives are changed as a result of their mentorship. Your mindset is more important than your location, situations and finances. With the right Mindset, success is inevitable.

Take the tools each writer gave and implement them immediately. Don't procrastinate because now is the time!

As a man thinketh in his heart so is he. Take the limitations off your mind.

GRADUATION IS RIGHT AROUND THE CORNER:

I was talking to a friend and business partner Wanda Honeyblue and she shared her experiences while pursuing her Bachelor of Art degree at Washington Bible College. There were eight other classmates in this accelerated program. It was a cohort. You stayed with the same classmates for two years. For two years Wanda played the same song while driving to class, Keep On Movin' by Soul II Soul.

Wanda would then walk into the class and make her daily announcement; graduation is right around the corner. The classmates would laugh at her, but she wouldn't let up off that affirmation because she was not just attending school, but she was working in a full-time, very demanding position. Wanda needed to convince herself that she could complete this class, work full-time and raise her three children. She endured a lot of late nights and it was difficult, but finishing was the focus. There are two types of courage, the courage to start and the courage to finish. The seven students laughed at her everyday BUT guess what? They had the same goal when they started but because Wanda worked on her mindset, she was the only one to finish the two-year course and graduate. The other seven students attended Wanda's graduation. They looked at her and said, "Wanda guess what, graduation is right around the corner."

True Wealth Starts in the Mind. Fix your mind and every goal, commitment, dream and affirmation will manifest.

Jeremiah 29:11, King James Version (KJV)

> *"For I know the thoughts that I think toward you, saith the LORD, thoughts of peace, and not of evil, to give you an expected end."*

Made in the USA
Columbia, SC
12 July 2022

63384057R00115